Praise for
IF THIS IS YOUR LAND, WHERE ARE YOUR STORIES?

"One of the most interesting non-fiction books of the year."
—*National Post*

"This is one wild, engaging ride."—*Toronto Star*

"J. Edward Chamberlin writes with astonishing originality
about the fluidity of human cultures—about our pressing need to
acknowledge the paradoxes and contradictory truths that are apparent
everywhere just under the surface of events. His book is a gift
that reads like the distillation of a lifetime of thinking
and personal experience."
—Erna Paris, author of *Long Shadows: Truth, Lies and History*

"Ted Chamberlin's book is delightful.
It tackles profound questions of cultural conflict, by reminding
us of our own songs and stories, revealing the extent to which
vocabulary and language enable us to know not only where we are
but who we are. They give meaning to our lives; in them we
are blessed by imagination, whether we realize it or not. And by
an understanding of the songs and stories of the peoples
who lie beyond our borders, or even within them, we can
truly know who we are, where we came from,
and what we—and they—may become."
—Thomas R. Berger, author of
One Man's Justice and *A Long and Terrible Shadow*

"Chamberlin dances between ideas, sources of ideas, anecdotes, giving the reader flashes of insight and glimpses of the world that are both new and profound. . . . [He] has made this tapestry so rich that it will be explored again and again."
—Hugh Brody, author of *The Other Side of Eden: Hunters, Farmers, and the Shaping of the World*

"There is no easy way to describe this remarkable book. Every page is a cascade of rich and original ideas, dazzling in their breadth and profound in their relevance. Baudelaire once identified horror of home as a great malady of the modern age. In a literary journey that takes us from the of the fires of the Gitksan to the forests of Africa, from the songs of cowboys to the poetry of shamans, from science to the realm of myth, Ted Chamberlin provides the cure."
—Wade Davis, author of *Light at the Edge of the World*

"This new book places us in the middle of the stories of indigenous peoples—from Canada to Africa to Australia—about themselves and the world. Chamberlin has become our literary bard through which these people are able to speak in their own voices. An extraordinary achievement, one made once in a generation. It is not only a book that all must read but, more importantly, one that we all must listen to."
—Sander L. Gilman, author of *Jewish Frontiers: Essays on Bodies, Histories, and Identities*

"Explores the idea of home through storytelling. This enthralling book touches on religion, nationalism, literature and mythology." —*The Vancouver Sun*

IF THIS IS YOUR LAND,

WHERE ARE YOUR STORIES?

 *Finding Common Ground*

J. Edward Chamberlin

VINTAGE CANADA

VINTAGE CANADA EDITION, 2004

Copyright © 2003 J. Edward Chamberlin Consulting Inc.

NATIONAL LIBRARY OF CANADA CATALOGUING IN PUBLICATION

Chamberlin, J. Edward, 1943–
If this is your land, where are your stories? : finding common ground
/ J. Edward Chamberlin.

Includes bibliographical references and index
ISBN 0-676-97492-9

1. Folklore—Social aspects. I. Title.

GR40.C42 2004   398'.09   C2003-905677-5

Pages 253 and 254 constitute a continuation of the copyright page.

www.randomhouse.ca

Text design: CS Richardson

Printed and bound in Canada

10 9 8 7 6 5 4 3 2 1

For Lorna

Contents

If this is your land, where are your stories?

Introduction

IT HAPPENED AT A MEETING between an Indian community in northwest British Columbia and some government officials. The officials claimed the land for the government. The natives were astonished by the claim. They couldn't understand what these relative newcomers were talking about. Finally one of the elders put what was bothering them in the form of a question. "If this is your land," he asked, "where are your stories?" He spoke in English, but then he moved into Gitksan, the Tsimshian language of his people—and told a story.

All of a sudden everyone understood . . . even though the government foresters didn't know a word of Gitksan, and neither did some of his Gitksan companions. But what they understood was more important: how stories give meaning and value to the places we call home; how they bring us close to the world we live in by taking us into a world of words; how they hold us together and at the same time keep us apart. They also understood the importance of the Gitksan language, especially to those who do not speak it.

The language sounded strange; it made no sense to most of the people there. But its strangeness was somehow comforting, for it reminded them that stories always have something strange about them, and that this is what first takes hold of us, making us believe. Recognizing the strangeness in other people's stories, we see and hear it in our own.

Other people's stories are as varied as the landscapes and languages of the world; and the storytelling traditions to which they belong tell the different truths of religion and science, of history and the arts. They tell people where they came from, and why they are here; how to live, and sometimes how to die. They come in many different forms, from creation stories to constitutions, from southern epics and northern sagas to native American tales and African praise songs, and from nursery rhymes and national anthems to myths and mathematics.

And they are all ceremonies of belief as much as they are chronicles of events, even the stories that claim to be absolutely true. We first learn this when we are very young; which is to say, we learn how to believe before we learn what to believe. It is what we believe—the second stage—that is at the heart of many of our current conflicts. We love and hate because of our beliefs; we make homes for ourselves and drive others out, saying that we have been here forever or were sent because of a vision of goodness or gold, or instructions from our gods; we go wandering, and we go to war. Whether Jew or Arab, Catholic or Protestant, farmer or hunter, black or white, man or woman, we all have stories that hold us in thrall and hold others at bay. What we share is the practice of believing, which we become adept at very early in our lives; and it is this practice that generates the power of stories.

We need to go back to the beginning. We all want to believe. We all *need* to believe. Every parent, every farmer, every builder, every cook knows this. We have to believe that the child will grow, or spring will come, or that the house will take shape, or the bread will rise. Stories and songs give us a way to believe, and ceremonies sustain our faith.

They also give us things to believe, which is a mixed blessing. The reality of our lives is inseparable from the ways in which we imagine it, and this closeness sometimes produces conflict and confusion. But it also produces some of our most durable myths, whose contradictory character seems to be part of being human and is certainly part of all cultures. The contradiction is inseparable from the nature of belief and the dynamics of believing, which always involve an element of strangeness and surprise.

Every story brings the imagination and reality together in moments of what we might as well call faith. Stories give us a way to wonder how totalitarian states arise, or why cancer cells behave the way they do, or what causes people to live in the streets . . . and then come back again in a circle to the wonder of a song . . . or a supernova . . . or DNA. Wonder and wondering are closely related, and stories teach us that we cannot choose between them. If we try, we end up with the kind of amazement that is satisfied with the first explanation, or the kind of curiosity that is incapable of genuine surprise. Stories make the world more real, more rational, by bringing us closer to the irrational mystery at its centre. Why did my friend get sick and die? Why is there so much suffering in the world? Whose land is this we live on? How much is enough?

And where is home? Home may be where we hang our hat, or where our heart is . . . which may be the same place, or maybe not. It may be where we choose to live . . . or where we belong, whether we like it or not. It may be all of these things or none of them. Whatever and wherever it is, home is always border country, a place that separates and connects us, a place of possibility for both peace and perilous conflict.

Except for the idea of a creator, there is no idea quite as bewildering as the idea of home, nor one that causes as many conflicts. It is a nest of contradictions. The late-twentieth-century image of the global village seemed to sound the death knell for home as a particular place, much as an earlier generation claimed to do for religion when they said God was dead. But the report of His death was an exaggeration (as Mark Twain once said when he read his own obituary in a newspaper); and so it is too with the idea of home. God has certainly not disappeared from the scene, and nor has Allah; the world seems to be getting larger, not smaller; and home is becoming more important, not less.

Can one land ever really be home to more than one people? To native and newcomer, for instance? Or to Arab and Jew, Hutu and Tutsi, Albanian and Kosovar, Turk and Kurd? Can the world ever be home to all of us? I think so. But not until we have reimagined Them and Us.

PART I *Them*

and Us

ONE

Babblers

I'LL BEGIN WITH BABBLING and doodling. We all begin there, after all. As we grow up, we grow out of the habit—or so we think. In fact, what we do is learn to dismiss others who haven't grown up exactly like us as incorrigible babblers and doodlers. And eventually the distinction becomes one of the ways we divide the world into Them and Us. There are those who doodle and do nothing. That's usually Them. And there are those who work, doing worthwhile things. Like Us. There are those who speak properly, again like Us; and those who babble, more or less meaninglessly, as They do.

By the meaningless sign linked to the meaningless sound we have built the shape and meaning of the world, said Marshall McLuhan. He was talking about how we represent ideas and things, which is another way of saying he was talking about babbling and doodling. Building shape and meaning is what we do in our stories and songs. They are built on the arbitrariness of words and images, which is to say they are built on sand; but they are rock solid as long as we believe in them. And that belief is founded on a sense of ceremony, a ceremony of shared belief. Such ceremonies often seem silly to those who don't grow up in them.

Table manners, for instance. I remember my early lessons in table manners. They seemed to me to give new meaning to meaninglessness. One day it was sitting up straight, which was, I thought, a waste of a well-made chair; another it was taking the piece closest to you when the plate was passed, which was stupid if you wanted a different piece. Then it was eating peas with a fork. My parents tried to convince me that mastering this skill would improve not only my current position but also my future prospects. I wasn't persuaded. Fingers were better. But since I was learning all about arbitrariness, I had an idea. I had seen Mary Kozak, the Ukrainian lady who came once a week to help my mother, eat her peas with a knife. This was even harder than eating them with a fork. So I thought I would try that at the dinner table. I sat up straighter than ever, spooned the portion of peas closest to me from the serving plate, and went to work with my knife. My father was not impressed. My mother said it was bad manners. I was ready. "But Mary Kozak eats that way," I replied.

Silence. My parents loved Mary Kozak, and I was counting on the fact that they wouldn't say anything disrespectful of her. But eating peas with a knife seemed to them sort of . . . well, "barbaric" would be a good word. Having failed the first time, I tried once again to balance the peas. Then, just as I thought I was winning the battle, my father said, "Learn to speak Ukrainian and you can eat peas with a knife."

Ukrainian seemed strange to me, and when I tried to speak it I sounded as if I were just babbling. It took me a while to realize that it was the verbal equivalent of eating peas with a knife. A ceremony, but someone else's.

When Europeans first arrived in southern Africa hundreds of years ago, the first people they met when they moved inland made strange noises. The newcomers reported that they sounded like animals. Their descriptions do not coincide with what we know of Bushmen speech, with its wide range of clicks and tones; and in fact, they were almost certainly yodelling, something the Bushmen did quite well. They were welcoming the strangers with music.

We can sympathize with the settlers, perhaps. It must have been like being greeted by bagpipes if you've never heard them. Most of us are not very good at listening to yodelling either, even though some musicologists say that music begins with the yodel, since the singing voice carries farther than speech. Still, to the settlers it sounded barbaric.

The word "barbaric" was first coined by the Greeks to describe the Persians, because they didn't speak Greek. They seemed to stammer when they spoke, sounding bar-bar-ic. They also looked different, behaved oddly, and their ceremonies were strange. They weren't necessarily uncivilized; they just weren't Greek.

Since then we have got into the habit of sharpening that distinction and dividing the whole world into the civilized and the barbaric, Us and Them, Somebodies and Nobodies. The Gitksan elder who asked, "If this is your land, where are your stories?" eventually had to go to court to try to convince the rest of us that the territory where his people had lived for thousands of years was his home. The case was called Delgamuukw, after one of the other elders (Earl Muldoe) who joined him in the suit; and during more than a year of testimony the Gitksan told their stories and sang their songs. But at the end of the day they didn't convince the judge, whose name was Allan McEachern, of anything other than their barbaric behaviour. Since the Gitksan ancestors had "no horses, no wheeled vehicles, no written literature," the judge said, they were "unorganized societies"—that was the legal phrase—"roaming from place to place like beasts of the field." Not "people" in what his nineteenth-century predecessors used to call "the true sense of the word." Nobodies.

In Mark Twain's novel *The Adventures of Huckleberry Finn,* when Huck was asked by Aunt Sally whether anybody had been hurt by the explosion on the Mississippi riverboat, he replied, "No'm. Killed a nigger." "Well, it's lucky," said Aunt Sally, "because sometimes people do get hurt." It seems that other people—people who don't write things down like we do, or speak like we do, or look like we do, or behave like we do, or work the land with horses and tractors like we do—can't get hurt. This was a tough bit of news for the Gitksan, who understandably claimed to have been quite severely injured when a whole bunch of people, looking a lot like me, came and settled on their land.

The settlers who arrived at the Cape of Good Hope were like that judge. They weren't sure the Bushmen were human at all, and they certainly didn't think the Bushmen could be hurt. Indeed, many settlers in the various "new" worlds to which they have wandered over the past millennia have had the same doubts. The Europeans who came to the Americas in the fifteenth and sixteenth centuries, for example, saw in the aboriginal people they met the social instincts of a more or less advanced herd of animals. Interestingly, there is evidence that *both* sides wondered about the other along much the same lines. Native people were just as astonished at the strangeness of the newcomers, and their stories tell of their uncertainty about just where *they* belonged in the great chain of being. So the misunderstanding works both ways. Each side thought the other did much worse than eat peas with a knife.

The natives had a lot of experience with strangers, and quite quickly figured out both the manners and the motives of this bunch. On the other side, the settlers began to wonder about their first impressions of the natives. Maybe they were not seeing what was right before their eyes. Maybe these native societies were more advanced, more human, than they first appeared. In the early 1500s a celebrated disagreement broke out, involving the fundamental question of whether the so-called New World people, misnamed "Indians," were to be considered human; whether their morals were those of a civilized society or barbaric; and—this was the crux of the matter for the settlers—whether their dispossession and enslavement were justifiable.

The dispute culminated in a formal debate held in Valladolid, Spain, between 1550 and 1551. At this distance it all seems rather legalistic, for it turned around a distinction between just and unjust "title," the sort of thing you would expect a lawyer to check before you bought a piece of property—which, of course, was exactly what the settlers were doing. Slaves were just as much property as land was, and often worth more. The character of the Spanish settlers' title to them was based on religious classification—specifically, whether they were Roman Catholic or not—and on whether they were won in a "just" war or were "properly" purchased.

The arbitrariness, or what Marshall McLuhan might call the meaninglessness, of all this should not be lost on us. These were some of the most learned scholars in Europe at the time. This was the Renaissance, after all, when learning was highly prized, and they were arguing about whether to believe such . . . well, such nonsense. Juan Gines de Sepulveda, a distinguished translator of Aristotle and the official historian for the Spanish court, argued that there was just cause in the Spanish conquest of the aboriginal inhabitants of the New World. The Indians were incapable of orderly living, he asserted, being disobedient by nature; they should therefore be subjected to rule, including enslavement. On the other side was Bartolomé de Las Casas, a settler and sometime priest, who insisted that the Indians were human and rational, and that their societies were highly developed, internally coherent, and continuously sustained by a set of habits and values to which all members of society adhered. Their enslavement, therefore, was unjustifiable.

National and international pressures overtook the disputants, and the essential issue of title to property—in this case, land and labour—remained unresolved. So did the question of where to draw the line between the barbaric and the civilized, and between the human and the non-human. We might think that these categories would have faded away, but no such luck. These days, they are routinely invoked to justify both terrorist acts and actions against terrorists; indeed, the category of terrorism itself is premised on a conviction that the world is divided into Them and Us. In saying "either you are with us, or you are with the terrorists," George W. Bush drew an old line in the sand. When 1960s demonstrators called police "pigs," or the old Chinese communist warriors talked about the "running dogs" of imperialism, each side was questioning the humanity of the other.

Let's go back and see if we can understand why. Human beings are often defined as animals who have language; so it is not surprising that the categories of the barbaric and the civilized first take shape along lines of language with the dismissal of a different language as either barbaric or so basic that it could not possibly accommodate civilized thoughts and feelings.

Sometimes, of course, the strangeness of a different language is taken to be an affirmation of *special* meaning and value, rather than of none at all. That's the connection between Ukrainian and table manners. We meet this often in the strangeness of sacred words, which many of us hold dear even though they may make little sense, at least in any ordinary way. From the sixth-century Arabic of the Qu'ran to the medieval Latin of the Roman Catholic liturgy, and from the ancient Hebrew of the Torah to the seventeenth-century English of the King James translation of the Bible, millions of people worship in languages they do not speak.

Here's a different example from an Aboriginal elder in Australia, greeting strangers the way the Bushmen did—with strangeness. "I tell'im, you don't belonga this country! You got no *tulku! Tjukurrpa!* Only I got'em *tulku*. We bin live along this country. We know this country. I don't know where you come from. You not boss for this place!" The speaker was Charlie Tjungurrayi, and the issues he raised were clear, even though the two Pintupi words that conveyed them—*tulku* and *tjukurrpa*—were not.

Tulku and *tjukurrpa* translate roughly as "song" and "dreaming," and together they represent all that is most significant about the relationship between aboriginal people and the land, between their past and the present, and between one and another. They are the beginning of an answer to the question "If this is your land, where are your stories?"

But Charlie Tjungurrayi did not translate them. What turned out to be most important about those two words was not their roughly translated meaning but the fact that they could not be translated. There's an old Italian pun on *traduttore* and *traditore*. The first means "translator"; the second "traitor."

Untranslatability is an ancient value, and one that my parents called upon when I tried to eat my peas with a knife. The Greek philosopher Plato once said that if we change the forms of story and song—he was especially concerned about music, but could have been talking about language—we change something fundamental in the moral and political constitution of a society. That's why he didn't want to change or translate them; and that's why others do.

For different languages and strange beliefs create conflict; and even if we avoid the conflict, they certainly encourage misunderstanding. Many Canadians, committed as they are to a bilingual country, have nonetheless made a career out of misunderstanding French and English (perhaps in order to avoid such conflicts); and although there are many countries dedicated to linguistic diversity, from Switzerland (with four national languages) to South Africa (with eleven), nobody claims it is easy. And the fault lines can be fatal, as Canada keeps being reminded.

Shouldn't we be trying to find common ground across cultures in language itself? In the Middle Ages, when you learned a language, people used the Latin word *habitus*, which meant you had the habit of it. Doesn't this suggest the obvious way to reconcile these conflicts: make sure everyone has the same habits, that they all speak in a certain way, behave in a certain way, believe in a certain way?

For all their political incorrectnesses, these are tough questions to answer. Why should language be an element of conflict when there is such a simple solution? One of the great stories across many cultures has to do with the proliferation of languages in the Tower of Babel, and the promise of a day when rivalries will be erased and conflicts eliminated in a common language. One problem, of course, is *which* language. The names of many aboriginal languages mean "the language," the one that anyone who wants to be civilized should speak; just as the names of many native nations—the Inuit (still called Eskimo in the United States), for example, or the Dene (who live from the northern tundra to the American southwest)—mean "the people." Not just any language, or any people; *the* language, and *the* people.

Language is the signature of both individual and collective identity, and even small differences of accent identify speakers of a community or a country. To give up these differences would be to give up something that seems essentially human, and that helps us understand who we are and where we belong. This cuts both ways. Those who do not speak a language, or do not speak it "properly," are made less certain of their identity by those who do. The Gitksan men and women who don't speak Gitksan are sometimes made to feel a little less like people (in the true sense of the word, of course). And yet language is the stuff of stories and songs, and we want them to be different. Strangeness and surprise are important to stories, and what could be stranger or more surprising than another language?

Let's come at this from a different direction. If diversity of languages is analogous to diversity of species, surely different languages should be nourished the way rare species are, by protecting their habitat. Doing this would mean protecting the land and the livelihood of the people who speak such languages. Languages spoken by only a few, like small pieces of land, would be just as precious as large ones; they would be like sacred sites. And while our limited success with all but a few endangered species might make us wonder about the practicality of this approach, isn't the principle of diversity a good one?

If we present the issue along evolutionary lines we come up with somewhat different questions. For instance, why should a particular language be preserved when another larger or stronger one seems ready to replace it? There are a goodly number of endangered languages around the world, and that's sad; but the age of the few remaining speakers and the generation gaps in their communities would suggest that English or Mandarin or Hindi or Turkish or one of the other dozen or so most widely spoken languages on the planet is going to take over sooner or later anyway, so why not now? Why not let things take their natural course and encourage the survival of the fittest language? What would be lost, other than a few species? Admittedly, there aren't that many species of languages, but there are lots of varieties, or dialects, within each family; and some of them, in a nice Darwinian flourish, might eventually become new species if the conditions were right.

The trouble is that the "right" conditions are often the product of force . . . as, of course, are the wrong conditions. The language that wins out is sometimes the one with the army. And we know that while some languages survive all sorts of violence, some do not. And others just slip away, less counted than spotted owls.

It all comes down to a simple question: why does it matter? One answer is that different languages may generate meaning differently, in which case what we are talking about is different ways of being in the world, different ways of being human—the barbaric way and the civilized way, a cynic might say. But we know that these are arbitrary categories, that there is no such thing as the barbaric and the civilized. Don't we?

The idea that we live our lives in language, and that we understand the world differently because we speak different languages, goes back a long way. During the seventeenth and eighteenth centuries, it was widely promoted. Gottfried Leibniz, who was the co-inventor of calculus, argued (in an essay on the improvement of the German language) that language was a fundamental determinant of thought and behaviour. By the late eighteenth century the idea had strong support from philosophers and critics and even poets. William Wordsworth, for example, came to the conclusion that language is "the incarnation of thought . . . not what the garb is to the body but what the body is to the soul"; while Samuel Taylor Coleridge, his friend and collaborator, took the other side of the argument and called language merely an instrument of thought, like a mathematician's slide rule.

For most of the twentieth century, the question was put by anthropologists like Franz Boas, who worked mostly on the northwest coast of North America. Boas startled some of his colleagues by insisting that learning indigenous languages was fundamental to their work. The earlier generation, represented by James Frazer (of *Golden Bough* fame), had stayed on the verandah writing English and reading Greek. But then linguists such as Edward Sapir and Benjamin Lee Whorf presented a detailed illustration of how languages shape not only our perception of things but the way we think and feel, determining the categories according to which we understand the world. This principle was given wide currency by Samuel Hayakawa in a popular mid-century book called *Language in Action*, and then made into a contemporary catchphrase by Marshall McLuhan: "The medium is the message."

Eventually, the notion that different languages shape different thoughts and feelings and even different forms of behaviour was given a modern scientific tag and called "linguistic relativity." Along with the postmodern enthusiasm for uncertainty and indeterminacy, it influenced postcolonial perspectives on the languages of colonized peoples. But long before both postmodernism and postcolonialism, it influenced my father when he said that I could eat my peas with a knife if I learned to speak Ukrainian.

The real impact of this line of thinking was negative, unfortunately, born of a conviction that aboriginal people should be taught European languages because their barbaric languages inhibited them from thinking and feeling in certain—which is to say, in civilized—ways. If one could change their language, it was argued, one could alter the way they thought and felt, changing them from childlike babblers and doodlers into adult citizens of a civil society. "Teaching an Indian youth in his own barbarous dialect is a positive detriment to him. The impracticability, if not impossibility, of civilizing the Indians of this country in any other tongue than our own would seem obvious," said the United States Commissioner of Indian Affairs in his annual report in 1887. Seeing language as the key to cognitive and cultural change turned out to be both the highest tribute to its power and the grimmest form of social engineering.

There were other conflicts that also came to the fore. One of the most stubborn had to do with babbling barbarians and the written languages of civilized people. We heard the judge dismiss the Gitksan because they had no written literature. Sometimes this dismissal takes a more polite, but no less pernicious, turn. Societies whose major forms of imaginative expression are in speech and performance are classified as oral cultures. Then they are praised for their naturalness and naïveté, while the rest of us lament the ways in which the sophistications of civilization have moved us away from a supposed oneness with the world, which these simple spoken languages represent, into the abstraction and alienation that come with the written word. Speaking and listening are simple and natural, we say; while writing and reading are cultivated and complex. We wonder how people in these oral cultures recall things so clearly and how they reflect on ideas without the benefit of writing; and then we decide they really don't, they merely remember formulae. Just like scientists, say a few dissenters . . . though we don't pay much attention to them, for after all these societies are "pre-scientific." So we celebrate their primitive consciousness, the kind that children display, and we remark on how it is resonant with an openness to experience that the rest of us lose as the prison house of written language closes in upon us. But we also know—and here we brighten up a bit—that with this new phase of our lives comes the compensation of self-reflexive intelligence, the intelligence capable of real thought. Our kind of thought. Modern thought.

It has become almost a truism that writing—alphabetic writing in particular—marked an evolutionary advance. Writing frees the mind for original, abstract thought, the argument goes, while oral cultures are imprisoned in the present, uninterested in definitions, unable to make analytic distinctions and incapable of genuine self-consciousness. Oral cultures understand the world in magical rather than scientific terms, and those in such cultures who have any acquaintance whatsoever with writing are agonizingly aware of what they are missing.

This kind of thinking—if we can call it that—encourages people to treat other societies with a blend of condescension and contempt while celebrating the sophistication of their own. And it entrenches the misconception that there *are* such things as "oral cultures" and "written cultures." Think about it. All so-called oral cultures are rich in forms of writing, albeit non-syllabic and non-alphabetic ones: woven and beaded belts and blankets, knotted and coloured strings, carved and painted trays, poles, doors, verandah posts, canes and sticks, masks, hats and chests play a central role in the cultural and constitutional life of these communities, functioning in all the ways written texts do for European societies. And, on the other hand, the central institutions of our supposedly "written" cultures—our courts and churches and parliaments and schools—are in fact arenas of strictly defined and highly formalized oral traditions, in which certain things must be said and done in the right order by the right people on the right occasions with the right people present. We are, all of us, much more involved in both oral and written traditions than we might think. And our stories and songs draw on the resources of both.

Still, the misunderstanding continues to cause problems. Let's return for a moment to the Gitksan. When they went to court to assert their claims to their aboriginal territory, they told the history of their people with all the ritual it required, for the stories and songs that represent their past—*ada'ox*, they call them—are about belief. On one occasion another elder, Antgulilibix (Mary Johnson), was telling her *ada'ox* to the court. At a certain point, she said that she must now sing a song. Judge McEachern was appalled; the request seemed to him to flaunt the decorum of his courtroom. He tried to explain how uncomfortable he felt at having someone sing in his court; he said it made him feel judicially embarrassed, sort of like my parents watching me eat peas with a knife. He tried to make the plaintiffs understand that this was unlikely to get him any nearer the truth that he was seeking. He asked the lawyer for the Gitksan whether it might not be sufficient just to have the words written down, and avoid the performance. Finally, he agreed to let Mary Johnson sing her song; but as she was about to start he fired his final salvo. "It's not going to do any good to sing it to me," he said. "I have a tin ear."

It was a stupid thing to say, for he wasn't the least bit interested in the song or its music anyway. But it also was a smart
thing to say; for he *did* have a tin ear, and he couldn't have heard
the music even if he *were* interested in it. Most of us go through
life assuming that we could make not only music but meaning
out of Mary Johnson's song. It is like assuming we can translate
tulku and *tjukurrpa*. For the Mary Johnsons of the world, it is a
sinister assumption. It is an assumption that understanding
sophisticated oral traditions comes naturally to the sympathetic
ear. It doesn't. Just as we learn how to read, so we learn how to
listen; and this learning does not come naturally.

Belligerent conservatives ask better questions than sympathetic liberals; that's why I am interested in the judge and his
tin ear and his tendentious "Why not just write it down?" He
said something else as he dismissed the case. He said he
believed Mary Johnson, but not her *ada'ox*. Another stupid
statement. Certainly none of *us* would have said it. But it picks
up a central question: Do we believe the singer or the song, the
teller or the tale? Far from being the product of twentieth-
century judicial arrogance, this question reflects an ancient
uncertainty that is at the heart of many great traditions of pro-
nouncement and performance in religion and politics and law.

It is impossible to expect that we will either educate our
imaginations in a very wide range of different languages and
different cultures, or else defer to them. We cannot always do
that, nor do we necessarily want to. We want to be able to say
"That rings false" on certain occasions without being called up
short like the judge for our ignorance or our stupidity. We may
sympathize with his predicament, but we don't want to exercise
his bad judgment. At the same time, we want our believing
to do justice to our *own* traditions of belief. We need a new
way of looking at stories and songs that balances the artifice
of their conventions with the naturalness —or the truth—of
their representation of the world.

A few years ago, the hereditary chief of the Cayuga proposed telling the cycle of stories and songs of his people—the
Great Law of the Haudenosaunee—in English. He was the
custodian of this most important of Iroquois oral traditions,
which it had taken him a lifetime to learn; but fewer than thirty
people understood it when he told it in Cayuga. So he wanted
to tell it in a language understood by the younger generation.
Many of the other elders were adamantly opposed; but he did
it anyway.

What should he have done? His intentions were certainly
honourable; but all cultures—including our own—have pro-
tocols governing ceremonies, and why shouldn't he respect
his? Was he being a traitor by translating, to recall that Italian
pun? Many Christians insist that only priests can prepare the
sacrament for communion. Judges must pronounce sentence,
in language of high formality. We use words out of another time
and place, and sometimes out of another language, for some of
our most important rituals—baptisms, weddings, funerals, ini-
tiations, excommunications, coronations. And many of us
would feel the ceremony had not really taken place—that what
was said and done was "untrue," or treacherous—were those
precise words not uttered on those occasions by those people.

Was the Cayuga chief a cultural vandal or a cultural hero?
Was the Great Law true when told in another tongue? Are
there gradations of truth? If so, what does that imply? Is a
poem spoken aloud by the poet "truer" than one read silently by
me? The implications of this could be very disconcerting . . .
and rather surprising to many people who have never entertained any thought of hearing John Milton or Emily Dickinson.
We understand our own traditions of performance less well
than we think.

Let's close this chapter with a look at one of the most influential attempts to find a way beyond this deadly conflict between

languages and cultures, Matthew Arnold's *Culture and Anarchy*. First published in England in 1869, it is a textbook example of the clash between Them and Us, and although its dedication to a particular set of values has been strongly criticized over the years, I think it has things to tell us. It exemplifies the categorization of peoples into the barbaric and the civilized, and the dismissal of babblers and doodlers. But it also opens a window onto the ways in which we use these categories, and might get beyond them.

In language that still resonates in contemporary public policy, Arnold spoke of the importance of "getting to know, on all the matters which most concern us, the best which has been thought and said in the world," and of the urgent need to create a society in which the "coarsely tempered natures" of the "barbarians and philistines" would be imbued with the "sweetness and light" of a truly cultivated, civilized community. He celebrated the authority of what he called "touchstones," stories and songs that embody the grace and power which inspire civilized conduct. In place of spiritual texts he proposed a secular canon of (mostly European) cultural touchstones which would provide the currency of a contemporary civil society.

So far, it sounds appallingly self-satisfied, not to mention more than a bit ethnocentric. It was. But Arnold was not sitting on some elegant English verandah when he wrote *Culture and Anarchy*. His country was in the midst of a deadly serious economic depression, in which differences of region and class and race were writ large; it had just embarked on major democratic reforms (epitomized by the Reform Bill of 1867, which dramatically extended the franchise) that were dividing an already deeply divided country. He felt the menace of mid-nineteenth-century European revolution, and the anarchic forces of social, economic and political change that seemed to be sweeping his world.

Many of us might recognize our own countries all too easily in Arnold's nineteenth-century England. Like us, he had reason to be worried about the stresses and strains that were threatening to break up his badly fractured nation, one that had been described as more like two nations by its sometime prime minister, Benjamin Disraeli (in the title of one of his novels, *Sybil, or the Two Nations*). Reacting to this, Arnold tried to redefine the categories of rich and poor that Disraeli had identified as the root of the problem.

That's where Arnold fell into the trap that categories always lay for us, for he simply replaced these with another set of oppositions, this time between those with culture and those without. Arnold recapitulated the encounter between the Greeks and the Persians with which we began this chapter. And he did a good job. No debate about cultural relativity and no discussion of national identity in the past century has been able to ignore Arnold's categorization of the world into civilians and barbarians. Culture and anarchy.

They have become hard-wired into our consciousness, both as meaningless and as meaningful as table manners. We are unlikely to get clear of them any time soon, but the *choice* between them is something else. It is a foolish choice between false alternatives. It is a choice between being isolated or being overwhelmed, between being marooned on an island or drowning in the sea. We will see the temptation to make this choice over and over again in this book, and each time I will try to show how dangerous and sometimes disastrous it can be.

For Arnold, it took the form of a choice between a society with civil ceremonies and one without, between listening to Mary Johnson sing her song in Gitksan and insisting that it be written down in English. A choice between having some sense of tradition, of convention, of table manners . . . and having none. Not different ones, but none at all. Or so he saw it. In some ways he was not so different from those first settlers. The spectre of anarchy haunted him like a nightmare.

But Arnold had a dream. It was a dream of a common culture, celebrating common meanings and values, with ceremonies that confirm a common purpose. It is the dream of many communities who want to affirm their collective identity along lines of region or race or gender or religion. Most importantly, it is the dream of ceremony itself.

This is the dream that came naturally to ancient societies and has shaped much of our modern world. And it is a dream that accommodates conflict. That's what Arnold didn't understand; and we have inherited his misunderstanding. Culture is *always* threatened by anarchy, as belief is by doubt. That's the essential nature of both culture and belief, and it is protected by ceremony. Conflict is at the heart of the way language works, and therefore the way stories work as well. Ceremonies are the custodians of this; and the real power of ceremony is not in achieving peace, as Arnold hoped, but in embracing contradiction. Pluralism is a danger not because it creates conflicts, as he thought, but because it masks them.

TWO

Doodlers

CULTURE AND ANARCHY was about ceremonies of belief, from constitutional texts to creation stories. Matthew Arnold stayed away from the former, because the United Kingdom did not have a constitution; and from the latter, because Darwin had just thrown the cat among the pigeons by seeming to set evolutionary theory into conflict with the book of Genesis. Had Arnold turned to them, he might have discovered how they embody the very conflicts and contradictions he was trying to puzzle out. For to an outsider, both creation stories and constitutions often sound like a lot of babble.

Let's look at one that brought the people of Montana into the United States in 1889. They came in with a constitution, a story that told who they were and why they belonged right there. It is interesting to compare the constitutions of the State of Montana and of the United States to illustrate how different kinds of communities in different times and places imagine themselves. Both begin with the words "We the people." The United States Constitution then identifies the specific purposes of government. Montana's constitution, on the other hand, begins this way: "We the people of Montana, grateful to God for the quiet beauty of our state, the grandeur of its mountains, the vastness of its rolling plain. . . ."

Why did they go on like this? "It would be possible to argue that they were simply being long-winded in a document which should be lean and concise," says the philosopher and politician Daniel Kemmis, who lives in Montana. In other words, that they were babbling. "But it could also be argued that they said not a word more than they had to say; and that what they had to say was that the way they felt about the place they inhabited was an important part of what they meant when they said 'we the people.'" Were their feelings about the place real or imagined? Well, they imagined the aboriginal people of that part of the plains right out of the picture; and that became a real fact of life. But they also imagined themselves into existence as a state of the union.

Imagine the Indians back into the picture for a moment. When the Siksika (Blackfoot) chief Isapo-muxika (Crowfoot) signed a treaty with the new Canadian government just a few years earlier and just a few miles north, he spoke for his people: "We are the children of the plains, it is our home, and the buffalo has been our food always." And he gave a prayer for "the mountains, the hills and the valleys, the prairies, the forests and the waters, and all the animals that inhabit them." Rhetorical babble? Perhaps. But he could have been writing the Montana constitution.

Other than constitutions, there are no stories more fraught with conflict than creation stories, especially since many societies believe two or more; and there are no stories that invite us to dismiss them quite as quickly. My first lesson in this came from my godmother, who with nice irony came from a settlement in Saskatchewan called Qu'Appelle. Whatsitsname. She was half-breed, and even more unsure of who she was and where she belonged. She told me how Indians came by a bridge across the Bering Strait from Russia; and she took me to see the dinosaur bones up in the badlands by Drumheller. "Were there Indians around then?" I asked. "Indians have been here forever," she answered, speaking words given to her by her Cree grandmother. These stories, of course, completely contradicted each other.

There was another creation story, and another kind of constitution, which my godmother believed as well. She had been told this one by her Scottish grandfather. Repeated from the Americas to Australia and across Africa, it was the settler's story. In this story, the new worlds were empty places. *Terra nullius* was the name in Latin, the old language of empire. The maps of the time give a picture of the place: rivers and prairies and mountains and lakes . . . with nobody there. "It's nobody's home," said the newcomers. "Therefore it's ours."

There *were* people there, of course, a lot of them, and this *was* their home. But the settlers quickly invented a myth of entitlement—a constitution, a creation story—to match their myth of discovery. In this story the aboriginal hunters and gatherers they met were just wandering about like beasts of the field, living idle lives on idle land. Certainly they were not farming, which is what civilized people did.

The way people behave—their way of life, or livelihood—often separates them even more than language does. We routinely divide people according to what they do, and whether they do the things that we think grown-up people, civilized people, ought to do.

There's something else involved in this. One of our oldest conflicts is between those who dream about things and those who do things, between those who sing songs and tell tales and those who raise meat, grow vegetables and cook supper. Doodlers and doers. The useless and the useful.

For millennia, societies have distinguished between the people who work in the yard and the people who play in the tower. In the yard, people supposedly make themselves useful doing things; in the tower they rise above all that and dream, uselessly.

We are constantly distinguishing between them, even though we know that they are two sides of the same coin. Hunters dance the hunt and dream it and draw it on the rock . . . and then they head out to the hills. Warriors fight because someone told them a story; and they sing as they go into battle.

Apollo is the god of both the lyre and the bow, of both song and struggle. The Taoist sage Chuang Tzu used to celebrate the ideal of *wu wei,* or active non-activity.

Still, the opposition between the useless and the useful has a hold on us. The classification of entire livelihoods as useless goes on every day, most obviously in the employment categories that disregard the work of raising families or of hunting for food. The classification of land as idle—land that is not used for agricultural purposes or owned by someone—has provided the basis for countless colonial adventures in the settlement of aboriginal territory; and it is still invoked to justify the encroachment on so-called wilderness lands.

The encounter between natives and newcomers all around the world for thousands of years has been premised on a distinction between doers and doodlers, typically identified as people who settle down and people who roam about. It has created conflicts for a very long time, much longer than any distinction between people on the basis of colour or creed. Let me give an example of the kind of misunderstanding upon which this distinction is based, and why it appeals to us.

Some years ago, I spent time in Australia working with aboriginal communities on land claims that were similar to those of the Gitksan. As I travelled I heard stories of an Englishman who was wandering about the country and writing down his impressions. His name was Bruce Chatwin; and *The Songlines* was the immensely popular book he eventually wrote. It was a tribute to the Aborigines of Australia as the original wanderers, and a praise song to a way of life Chatwin could only dream about, one that he had lost in childhood. A life of perpetual doodling. Good doodling, mind you. Spiritual doodling. Doodling in the outback, where everything is true and beautiful and good. But doodling nonetheless.

Think about it. Aborigines, who know the names of every plant and the location of all the water holes, as perpetual nomads? Europeans in a place ten thousand miles from home, as settlers? It doesn't make sense. For millennia, farming people have roamed around the world looking for new places and dreaming of the home they left behind, moving on after a generation or so to other new places. And we call these people—Chatwin's people, my people, Us—"settlers"? The other people, the indigenous people who have lived in the same place for tens of thousands of years . . . we call Them "wanderers"? It's hard to imagine a more cockeyed set of catagories.

The truth is that We are the nomads and They are the settlers. But thanks to the likes of Bruce Chatwin (and every generation has its designer vagabonds), we project the confusion onto those whose nomadic lives we envy . . . and whose land we often want. Chatwin's story, like that of Columbus, had little to do with Aborigines and a lot to do with his own anxieties and ambitions. Chatwin was looking for home and he found it thousands of miles away in an ideal of wandering, just as his ancestors had for hundreds of years. Columbus was looking for India, and he found it in the people he called Indians. This reminds me of Majorcan storytellers who always begin by saying "It was and it was not"; indeed, I am not sure that we don't believe stories like this, even—or especially—when we know they are not true. This possibility may help us understand the appeal of stories that are so wrong-headed. They celebrate habits of belief, not a set of events.

The story Chatwin tells is a familiar one to many of us. It is nicely incorporated into our contemporary image of stability and security, the family farm . . . always with too many children to support, so that sooner or later they must go out and find new places to farm, displacing another group of people who have been there since time immemorial. But the story goes back over ten thousand years to the Neolithic migrations of agricultural peoples; it is found in both the Bible and the Qu'ran, each representing traditions of agricultural enterprise.

It is there in Xhosa and Zulu praise songs, and in the Bhagavadgita. It is shared by herders and farmers of all times and places and races and creeds, for whom what they do and how they do it defines what civilization is all about. And it draws a clear line between Them and Us, or between childlike, wandering doodlers and civilized, settled doers.

For those of us who grew up during the 1940s and 1950s in North American families, the guide to what was civilized was provided by a series of books written by Will and Ariel Durant called *The Story of Civilization*. The Durants were not the denizens of privileged institutions; they taught recent immigrants at the Labor Temple and the People's Institute in New York, and their criteria were not exclusively European. But they *were* agricultural. In the first volume, setting out the frame of reference, Will Durant considered the Middle East, North Africa, China, Japan and, most of all, India. "The conditions of civilization," he said, are "economic provision, political organization, moral traditions and the pursuit of knowledge and the arts. It begins where chaos and insecurity end." In other words, to be civilized is to settle down and start farming.

For their part, of course, aboriginal societies thought of themselves as the civilized ones. "There goes the neighbourhood," they said when they saw the settlers arriving. They believed the place was indisputably theirs. They had stories of being there forever, and of how the rivers and prairies and mountains and lakes with which they shared dominion over the land came into being. The so-called settlers seemed like the wanderers to them, strange presences. Around 1840, a British explorer named George Grey wrote about the Australian Aborigines' impression of the Europeans who were moving onto the land. He reported that since the Aborigines had no thought of ever leaving their land, they also had no notion of other folk leaving theirs. "When they see white

people suddenly appear in their country, and settl[e] themselves down in particular spots, they imagine that they must
have formed an attachment for this land in some other state of
existence, and hence conclude the settlers were at one period
black men, and their own relations." White is the colour of
death, after all.

In the previous chapter, I talked about the false choice that is so
often presented to us, the choice between being marooned on
an island and drowning in the sea. Stories and songs can frus-
trate that choice if we let them. That's their great gift to us.
They do so by constantly negotiating between belief and
doubt, and between reality and the imagination, finally
embracing both in a contradiction that brings us back to our
babbling and doodling days.

Let me give an example of how this works. It is from the
best-known of all cowboy songs, "Home on the Range."
Composed over 125 years ago, its opening rhyme is still so
familiar to many in North America that it seems like a member
of the family: "O give me a home, where the buffalo roam."
Listen to the rhymes: "home" and "roam." Although bound
together by similar sounds, their senses pull in completely
opposite directions. Settling down and wandering. It's hard to
imagine a more basic human opposition, or a more fundamental condition in the Americas, or indeed in Africa, Asia,
Europe or Australia for that matter. Our imaginations take this
in every time we sing this song, and we remember these lines
not because they tell a single truth but because they tell two
contradictory ones.

Of course, I wasn't thinking about any of this when I tried
to balance peas on my knife. I was six years old, living on the
prairies in the west of Canada, and I had a friend who knew
how to yodel. Coming from Vancouver, where I was born,
my contribution was *"Kla-how-ya, Tillicum,"* a phrase in

Chinook, the language that had developed over a couple of hundred years of contact between natives and newcomers on the West Coast. The local newspaper had started the Tillicum Club, with a badge and a bookmark, and they said it was a good way of greeting people. So every day we would parade along the street, yodelling and yelling. Sometimes I would add one of the songs I had heard on the radio, like "Home on the Range."

We must have been a strange sight. But for a youngster on the prairies in the 1940s, the whole world seemed strange. The ghosts of the past—cowboys and Indians, the broncs and the buffalo that were part of their story—were all around. They would come to life every summer in the Calgary Stampede, one of the great rodeos of the West, and in the "Indian Days" that accompanied it when riders from the tribes of the Blackfoot Confederacy would bring their horses into town, decked out in the marvellous bead and leather work of their traditional regalia.

Aside from that summertime carnival, cowboys and Indians came to most of us in stories and songs. One of the first collections of folk songs in the Americas was John Lomax's *Cowboy Songs and Other Frontier Ballads*, published in 1910. And the speeches of Indian leaders like Chief Joseph and Sitting Bull and Chief Seattle and Tecumseh were the stock-in-trade of schools. Indeed, from the early 1800s, the speeches of Indian chiefs were quoted in encyclopedias around the world to illustrate the purest form of civil ceremony and poetic power.

Along with the speeches, of course, there were the hair-raising stories. I grew up with tales about the Sioux scalping settlers and leaving their mutilated bodies for the birds. But I also grew up with my grandfather telling about Sitting Bull, who was his contemporary, asking:

What treaty that the whites have kept has the red man broken? Not one. What treaty that the whites ever made with us red men have they kept? Not one. When I was a boy the Sioux owned the world. The sun rose and set in their lands. They sent 10,000 horsemen to battle. Where are the warriors today? Who slew them? Where are our lands? Who owns them? What white man can say that I ever stole his lands or a penny of his money? Yet they say I am a thief.

The contradictions didn't bother me. Like all children, I liked them. In fact, I wouldn't have recognized any story that didn't have some. I was learning something fundamental about stories, and how to believe them . . . for we do have to *learn* how to believe. "It was, and it was not," the storytellers of Majorca begin; and in my tradition they open with "Once upon a time," conjuring up both time immemorial and bedtime. Among the herders and hunters of southern Namibia and the Kalahari where I have been working for the past few years, the word |*garube* is used ("|" indicates a soft click made at the front of the mouth); it means "the happening that is not happening." "Infinity is a place where things happen that don't," say mathematicians. The novelist E. L. Doctorow was once criticized for bringing characters together in his historical novel *Ragtime* who could not possibly have met in real life. "They have now," he replied. *Did the Greeks Believe in Their Myths?* asks the French classicist Paul Veyne in the title of his book. Yes and no, he answers. "Believe it and not"—rather than "believe it or not"—is the challenge of every metaphor, of every myth, of every religion, of every community. When we forget that challenge, myth degenerates into ideology, religion into dogma, and communities into conflict.

With cowboys and Indians there was another contradiction, which is why I want to stay with their stories and songs for a while. The cowboys—who invariably looked like Us—were the perpetual wanderers, the unmannerly buffoons; the Indians—who were unmistakably Them—were always at home, defending their lands with a freedom fighter's fierceness. In fact, in many of the stories and songs, cowboys were portrayed a lot like the wandering Indians of the popular imagination; and the Indians were a lot like the settlers in their attitude towards home. This may give us a clue to the extraordinary appeal of these old tales. And perhaps it is why we often sided with the cowboys. Bruce Chatwin certainly would have.

Later, we will look more closely at the Indians. But what of those cowboys? Were they really Us? My grandfather was a cowboy for a while, running twelve thousand head of cattle in the foothills of southern Alberta, but by the time I knew him he was an old man sitting in the back garden telling stories. Maybe the appeal of cowboys has more to do with that conflict between wandering and settling down, and between the useless and the useful, than it does with their B-movie fights with the Indians.

The first cowboys in the Americas were in the Caribbean. This always surprises me, though it's obvious when you think about it. In his second voyage to the New World, Columbus brought twenty-four stallions, ten mares and a significant number of cattle. The animals thrived, and in remarkably short order a surplus of wild cattle roamed the region, while horsemen adapted Spanish equestrian techniques and equipment to hunt and herd them. As settlement spread to the mainland, horses and cattle moved across the continent. Along with them came the cowboys, roaming with the animals and fiercely independent of those who were beginning to settle down on the plains. They became the *gauchos* of Argentina, Uruguay and the Rio Grande do Sul region of Brazil; the *llaneros* of Venezuela and Colombia; the *vaqueros* of northern Brazil, northern Mexico and the Spanish southwest; the *huasos* of Chile; and the cowboys of the western United States and Canada.

They were more or less self-sufficient, displaying a contempt for those who lived in the towns, combined with envy or nostalgia for the comforts that settled folk enjoyed. They disdained the laws of the country, respecting only those enforced by the land itself, and by the weather; and their legendary freedom was dependent on their working for twelve to fourteen hours a day (unless they were riding night herd, when it would be all the time except for breakfast and dinner), seven days a week, months at a time. They developed a fairly simple set of habits which defined their place on the plains. They had no home. They owned no land. And they never would. Period.

How is it, then, that their way of life became the envy of so many people in the years following their heyday in the eighteenth and early nineteenth centuries, the very years when settler ideals of home and native land were being fashioned and when property of all sorts was highly prized? Part of it was the apparent innocence of cowboy life, with its closeness to nature and its distance from the artifices of towns and cities; part of it was the escape from routine and the freedom from those very same ties to place and community that were then being celebrated, the ties that bind. Those of us who wanted to be cowboys when we grew up didn't simply want to be part of colonial expansion or frontier violence. We wanted something else, something much more deeply engrained not in the history of the West but in the imaginations of children. We wanted lives that were both determined and free, both defined by necessities and defiant of them, both middle class and outcast. We wanted to be "bound to go," in the blues phrase that catches the contradiction better than anything. And knowing in our souls that we lived in some story or another, we wanted to live in *that* story. Cowboy songs and stories were our constitutions.

And they taught us about contradictions, as the useful and the useless rode out together. Cowboys were gloriously extravagant, at least according to their stories and songs, routinely spending wages from six months on the trail in as many days in town, and wearing clothes and gear that displayed a love of show— boots, spurs, hats, chaps, shirts, saddles, bits and bridles. And yet they developed skills in riding and roping, in herding and hunting down strays, that were models of economy and efficiency, and sometimes of astonishing grace. Some of these you could see on display in the movies, if you couldn't make it to a rodeo or a stampede.

Cowboys also never made a clear distinction between work and play, and even their singing fell between. Most of them believed that songs, or at least the sound of a human voice, helped settle cattle—a notion that is still current in dairy barns around the world—and at night especially they would sing to the herd. When they ran out of tunes, they would launch into a litany of profanities often contradicted by some religious humming; or they might recite the words on a coffee label or a can of condensed milk. And during the day, they would whoop and yell and hoot and holler to move the herd along. As far as I can tell, nobody ever actually *heard* a cowboy yodel *"yippee-ki-yi-o,"* as one famous song has it; but they might have. Cowboys worked and played with language, as they worked and played with everything else, creating a lexicon of technical terms lovingly twisted and translated into cowboy lingo: *criollo* was applied to cattle and horses as much as to people of mixed blood; *reata* migrated to "lariat," *vaquero* to "buckaroo," and *dar la vuelta* (wrapping the end of a rope around the saddle horn) to "dally"; a "willow" was a range mare, a "waddie" a cowboy riding one (or anything else, for that matter), and a "slow elk" a cattle beast poached by a waddie out of work.

From the beginning, horses and cowboys were inseparable. Cowboys depended on horses for their livelihood and for their lives. But once again it was the wildness of these horses, their dangerous unpredictability, that seemed to be part of their appeal. Cowboys would boast about horses that "could pitch more ways than a Chinaman could write," and many early cowboy songs celebrated bucking broncos, especially unridable ones like the Strawberry Roan and Midnight the Unconquered Outlaw.

In their counterculture way, cowboys admired Indians, the great horsemen of the plains, even as they sometimes feared them. They shared a horse culture that went deep into their souls. They shared too a hunter's sense and sensibility. Like Indians, cowboys reserved most of their resentment for settlers, or "nesters" as they were called, and for the soldiers who came to force them off their land or fence them in. The contempt for farmers that was part of my upbringing—the most insulting thing you could say about someone was that he was a dumb farmer—was the reverse of our admiration for cowboys, and of course equally caught up in contradiction.

Fences and farmers would ultimately do in both cowboys and Indians. Fences especially. "Don't fence me in" became a catchy refrain for good reason. In the words of one Alberta cowboy, "Barb wire is what ruined this country. At first we could keep it cut pretty well, and use the posts for firewood, but it got so, after a while, they were putting up the damned stuff faster than a guy could cut it down. . . . When I saw that I said to myself, I says, 'This country's done for'—and you see now I was right."

At the end of the day, cowboys and Indians were both denounced as barbarians, beyond the pale of settler societies. Indeed, in their apparent acceptance of uncertainty and insecurity they seemed completely beyond the pale of civilization. Cowboys had nothing, only songs. We were about to do our best to ensure that Indians had nothing either, except maybe speeches. And neither of them *did* much, at least as far as we could see. They were the doodlers of our world, our heroes in a conflict between a useful future and the useless past.

Let me illustrate this in another way, with a story about horses. Indian horses. The Navajo have lived in the Southwest for generations, hunting and gathering and more recently planting crops and grazing stock. The region is very dry, and their grasslands are vulnerable to drought and overgrazing. But the sky comes right down to the earth there, and up in the mountains, spirits dwell.

The Navajo came to that region about five hundred years ago from the northern tundra where their Athapaskan-speaking cousins still live, and like all travellers they brought some of their own ways and adopted some new ones, taking up methods of cultivating the land, the arts of weaving and some of their religious rituals from the Pueblo; the keeping of sheep for food and clothing, and the crafts of silver and turquoise from the Zuni and the Spanish; and horses, too, probably also from the Spaniards—though there is a persistent belief among some of the Indian tribes that the ancient horses of the plains never became extinct, and that the native peoples of the West were familiar with horses before the Spanish came. Whatever the case, horses have long been important to the Navajo.

When settlers moved west in the nineteenth century, the Navajo were forced off their lands by Kit Carson, operating under instructions from the United States government. A few years later, after being held in a hell-hole refugee camp called Bosque Redondo, they were allowed to move back. The next threat to the Navajo came not from frontier greed and corruption and the apparently boundless violence of American law and order, but from some enlightened and well-intentioned liberals.

Towards the end of the nineteenth century, after the trauma of the Civil War, attention in the United States turned to the Indian question. From the perspective of the Indians, of course, it was essentially a non-Indian question; but that was not how it was interpreted by even their most dedicated friends, who saw tribal allegiance as a useless bit of nostalgia that was interfering with their acceptance of the modern values of individualism (which flowed from ideas of freedom) and of property ownership (a little less idealistic, to be sure, but linked to ideas of independence and opportunity). The solution was to break up that allegiance by severing each community's attachment to its homeland, or to the reserves to which many had been moved.

The results were breathtaking and brutal. Prompted by a curious compact of earnest zealots and avaricious scoundrels—the former wanted the Indians' soul, the latter wanted their land—the government passed what was called the General Allotment Act in 1887. The act abolished tribal control over land tenure and opened up their lands for individual ownership, first of all by Indians and, in short order, by unscrupulous whites. In a terrible irony, this act was one of a group of so-called homestead acts that were intended to fulfil admirably democratic ideals, providing nineteenth-century immigrants with an opportunity for advancement independent of class—exactly the same thing that college education was designed to provide for their twentieth-century counterparts. But for the Indian people it provided nothing except misery. It was appreciatively referred to by President Theodore Roosevelt as "a mighty pulverizing engine to break up the tribal mass."

And it did its job, dispersing about 90 million acres of land formerly reserved for tribes, and leasing much of the remaining lands for grazing—or more usually, for overgrazing—by white ranchers. In concert with the suppression of Indian languages, traditions and ceremonies, it also broke the spirit of many Indians and undermined the structure of many tribal governments.

Yet fifty years later, the tribes were still there, indomitable and enduring, though often in wretched circumstances. Concerned by their destitution and dispossession, and by the appalling health conditions, severe educational limitations and grotesque administrative arrangements that prevailed in many Indian communities, the Department of the Interior commissioned a report from the Institute for Government Research (later known as the Brookings Institute). Directed by Lewis Meriam, it provided an exhaustive catalogue of the relentless dispossession of Indian land, the systematic destruction of Indian tribes and the brutal dislocation of Indian people. It was filled with righteous (and well-researched) indignation about the breaches of trust that had characterized the administration of Indian affairs. It was harsh in its criticism of the land allotment policy that had been in place for a half a century, and it recommended the re-establishment of tribal governments with control over land and resources. It was eloquent in its celebration of the values of community and of place, and the interdependence of spiritual and material values in both native and non-native society.

It was also incorrigibly utilitarian in the remedies it proposed. So when it came to describing the situation of the Navajo, one of the largest and most powerful of the tribes, it forgot about their horses. Actually, it didn't quite forget. It dismissed their horses in one paragraph in its nearly nine hundred pages. The paragraph was titled "Worthless Horses."

Worthless? These were the horses that worked the land, pulled the wagons, carried the men and women, and herded the stock. They had hunted the buffalo on the northern plains; and everywhere, from the Navajo to the Nez Perce, they held the imagination. That was their real value. For these were horses that grazed wild on the grasslands, defying the immediate demands of subsistence and signifying not just prestige but a kind of sovereignty. Seen in this light, a horse became its own reason for being—not a convenience or a commodity but a covenant, a ceremony linking Navajo survival with Navajo power. A covenant between fresh air and freedom to breathe. A ceremony of belief in truth and beauty and goodness. All this completely confounded the authors of the Meriam Report. They did not understand that horses could be both useful and useless, and that was why they were so important to the Navajo people.

Unlike many government reports, this one was acted upon. The Indian Reorganization Act, landmark legislation under the New Deal, was passed in 1934. It was unquestionably on the progressive side of things, and called for the revitalization of local communities and the development of local economies. For the reform-minded officials working with the Navajo, this meant new grazing practices to reverse fifty years of abuse by white leaseholders and to sustain the sheep and the goats that were a staple of Navajo life. Accordingly, a livestock reduction program was proposed.

Oscar Wilde once said that art has two kinds of enemies: those who dislike it, and those who like it rationally. The second, he insisted, are the real menace. Something of this menace now faced Navajo horses, and therefore the Navajo. The livestock reduction proposal was based on what were called "sheep units." Everything was calculated in sheep units . . . especially worthless horses. On average, a horse eats as much grass as five sheep; so each horse was now worth five sheep.

The Navajo knew the state of their grasslands and the need for restrictions. They had survived as a people for thousands of years, and for several hundred in the drylands of the Southwest. But they refused to have their sense of who they were and where they belonged determined by a diminished, impoverished vision that saw everything reducible to sheep units. The Indian agent with the Navajo at the time, Reeseman Fryer, said later that he thought that single phrase—"sheep units"—inflicted a deeper wound on the Navajo than almost anything else in those times of suffering and sacrifice. The federal government directed the Navajo to round up their five-sheep-unit horses, and sell or destroy them. The Navajo said no.

The refusal of the Navajo to embrace the livestock reduction program and its sheep units had to do with more than just horses. But horses were at the heart of it, representing Navajo resistance to those who deemed horses nothing more than a worthless indulgence, an offence against the virtues of social utility and economic morality that informed the restructuring programs of the American New Deal.

The reasons for this stand-off, and for many similar ones, are often laid at the door of ignorant officials. If only those responsible for introducing these changes had known more about the Navajo, or about tribal governments, or about land management, or about horses, we say. But in fact they knew a great deal about all of these. They knew the Navajo, and Navajo country. The man most responsible for the initiatives that led to the restoration of tribal government and the land conservation policies and those pernicious sheep units was John Collier, who became Commissioner of Indian Affairs in the 1930s. He was an articulate social activist who had taught at the People's Institute in New York, lived among the Pueblo, and was deeply committed to self-determination for native peoples and respect for the diversity of their cultures. So what was the problem? Why couldn't John Collier get it right?

Collier was a decent, well-intentioned man. But while he seemed to misunderstand the Navajo, what he actually misunderstood had less to do with the Navajo than with his own society and his own stories. He didn't understand the importance of the contradictions at the heart of all that we hold most dear. Preoccupied with the Navajo, he didn't recognize the common ground they shared with his own culture.

He should have known better. He should have known about horses being important to people in ways that went well beyond ordinary utility. He should have known because it was right there in his own stories and songs. He had read widely, and he had listened to Navajo stories about horses and heroes and the knowledge they provided of how to keep the everyday at bay; but he had forgotten about the stories he knew best. In the program of Great Books that he helped develop though the New York Public Library and the People's Institute, there were a lot of stories about worthless horses. This program was in fact much less narrowly conceived than many of its successors, and had its origins not in elite towers but in the yards of the late-nineteenth-century British industrial reform movement, where men and women knew all about dreaming. It was intended for what the radio and television industry would call broadcasting rather than narrowcasting, and in many ways its ambitions were not unlike those of Oprah's Book Club. Some of the books were lighthearted, others much heavier-going; and along with a wide range of literary, historical, philosophical, natural and social scientific texts from Europe, they included many works from other cultural traditions, such as classical Chinese and Persian poetry, the medieval *Morte d'Arthur* and the Qu'ran.

There was a story among those books about a classic conflict between barbarians and civilized people. Except this time it was the Greeks, not the Persians, who were the barbarians. After the siege and sacking of the city of Troy, the Greek hero Achilles drags the corpse of the Trojan commander Hector in the dust behind his horses to the funeral pyre of his friend Patroclus, whom Hector had killed. Then he leaves Hector there in the open to be eaten by dogs and birds. But other powers are at work to maintain some ceremony. The goddess Aphrodite anoints Hector's body with ambrosia, and Apollo keeps the sun away to save it from rotting, until finally on Zeus's command Achilles delivers up the body to Hector's father.

"Thus held they funeral for Hector, tamer of horses." These are the final words of Homer's epic *The Iliad*, a story from the crossroads of Europe and Asia and Africa, where misunderstandings between civilians and barbarians were the order of the day. They hold out a promise of dignity in the face of defeat and death. Not "Hector, worth five hundred sheep units," but "Hector, tamer of horses."

Oh, but that all happened such a long time ago, we say. And such a long way off. But of course it didn't. Hector the Homeric hero is the Indian cowboy who just arrived in the pickup truck. Long before I knew about Homer's Hector, I wanted to be like him, a tamer of horses. And I even knew a cowboy named Hector, riding the rodeo circuit in the Kootenay and Columbia River basins. Like his namesake, he got into a nasty fight over someone else's woman, and he got dragged about in the dirt a lot. When a Brahma bull he rode for all of two and a half seconds caught him from behind and tossed him back up over the chute in Coeur d'Alene, the rodeo announcer had a far-fetched figure of speech ready, just like Homer. He said that he'd gotten his oil checked.

Yet Collier and his colleagues didn't see all this. Maybe they were mesmerized by their colleague Will Durant, teaching across town at the Labor Temple and insisting that civilization begins when chaos and insecurity end, with the equivalent of sheep units. In any case, they could not see the parallels between the Navajo saga and the story told over twenty-five hundred years ago, which also celebrated the irrational and the unreasonable and the inexplicable as central parts of our lives; while the Navajo themselves, who did not know Homer but had their own scholars and storytellers drawing on tales remarkably like *The Iliad*, understood that horses count for something more than sheep. They recognized that the choice they were being offered—between useless horses and useful sheep—was a false one, like the choice between being marooned on an island and drowning in the sea. They insisted that while their horses might well be worthless—to claim otherwise was to risk falling into the cost-accounting of sheep units—they were also priceless.

THREE

There Goes the Neighbourhood

"MES DEN HEP *tavas a-gollas y dyr,*" goes an old Cornish proverb. "The tongueless man gets his land took." For many people, finding a voice—and a language—in which to tell their stories has been part of the problem. That, and finding someone to listen.

Australia's founding legislation, passed in 1901, provides a kind of parable for a situation that is commonplace around the world. "In reckoning the numbers of people of the Commonwealth, or of a State, or other part of the Commonwealth," it stated, "Aboriginal natives shall not be counted." This section was not amended until 1967; and although it was surrounded by complicated legal fictions within which it had a kind of justification, in the final analysis it represented a simple belief: aborigines are not to be counted because they do not count. Huck Finn couldn't have put it better. Many groups will recognize the logic. Only in 1929 did women in Canada finally win the right to hold public office in a case that became known as the Persons Case, because before that women were not, to put it in constitutional terms, people in the true sense of the word. In Dari, one of the main languages of Afghanistan, the same word refers to "child" and "son"—so when someone asks how many children you have, often enough girls don't count. But before we get feeling too superior, we should remember how highly gendered the English language still is.

Behind the Australian constitution lay another story, which I mentioned in the last chapter. In the beginning—that is, a mere two hundred years ago—there was nothing at all in Australia.

This was the seafaring theology of the first Europeans to arrive there in the eighteenth century. It was *terra nullius,* a place where there was nobody. Or perhaps I should say nobodies.

The newcomers' response was to proclaim sovereignty and thereby claim the land. That's what the British immediately did, at first in 1768 when Captain Cook sailed up the east coast waving the flag; and later on January 26, 1788, at Sydney Cove, when Governor Arthur Phillip planted the Union Jack. According to the principles of both natural and international law at the time, occupation and settlement of "uninhabited" country brought into force the laws of the colonizing power, including property laws. The other ways of acquiring sovereignty and thereby land were by conquest, by sale or by cession (usually in the form of a treaty). Whatever the method, in terms of British settlement this meant that ultimate title to all lands in the colony became vested in the Crown from the moment sovereignty was proclaimed, and all proprietary rights would subsequently be traceable to Crown grant. This is what is called underlying Crown title, and as we shall see it is a very useful story to have come up with.

There was general agreement that colonizing powers had not only a right but also a *duty* to occupy lands that would otherwise lie idle and, accordingly, that hunter-gatherer societies roaming over their vast lands had to make way for those who would cultivate the soil. No worries, for as the seventeenth-century English philosopher John Locke had assured everyone, "There can be no injury where there is no property." And nobody to get hurt. The Swiss jurist Emmerich de Vattel, in a book called *The Law of Nations* first published in the eighteenth century and widely translated and read over the next hundred years, argued that people "cannot exclusively appropriate to themselves more land than they have occasion for and which they are unwilling to settle and cultivate." Since it seemed obvious that the Aborigines—the same people who weren't there—were neither settled on nor cultivating the land, this became another powerful argument to justify their dispossession.

It still is, all around the world. In Asia, in Africa, in Europe as well as in Australia and the Americas, the discounting of other people according to arbitrary categories of entitlement continues, whether on the basis of livelihood or lineage, of creed or colour. The logic is that they don't have any of whatever it is: no farms, no written history, no faith, no get-up-and-go. So they are forced to do just that, get up and go.

Not all constitutions discount people, of course; but in one way or another they do define a community, and claim land. And overall, our contracts with each other, our covenants with the land, and the canticles we sing to celebrate our lives—our folk songs and national anthems—are still wracked with the old anxieties about civilian and barbarian, native and newcomer, the metropolis and the hinterland, farmer and hunter; and they are riddled with the deceptions and deceits by means of which we manage these dichotomies. A lot of our contemporary literature seems to be in the business of confirming this theatre of Them and Us, with its chronicles of difference and historical distress.

Some years ago I organized a symposium on Aboriginal Self-Determination at the University of Toronto with the national aboriginal organization in Canada, the Assembly of First Nations. It was designed to commemorate the anniversary of a conference that had taken place in 1939, jointly sponsored by the University of Toronto and Yale University, called "The North American Indian Today." At that earlier gathering, there were only about a dozen Indians. Ours was different; but with grim irony, it coincided with a crisis over Mohawk land near Oka, Quebec, where the townspeople wanted to turn the land into a golf course. The Mohawk objected; things got nasty; a police officer was killed, and the Canadian army was sent in. A lot of people, both aboriginal and non-aboriginal, came to our conference to see where things were going.

We had asked George Watts, the chief of the Nuu-chah-nulth on the northwest coast, to act as moderator. On the first day, a panel of experts, mostly aboriginal, gave their opinions. At the end of the discussion Chief Watts asked them to sum up, and when they had finished, he suggested that what they said could have been put in six words: "This is my land. Fuck off."

There is much to be said for bluntness like this. But the fact is that if "fuck off" is the only story we can come up with, we're all in trouble. George Watts knows that. He also knows, as we all do, that these words, or words much like them, can be heard in almost any conflict between cultures around the world right now: Palestinian and Israeli, Tibetan and Chinese, Albanian and Kosovar, Chechnyan and Russian, Ulster Protestant and Irish Catholic, black Zimbabwean and white . . . the chorus is deafening.

In these situations, both civil and uncivil disobedience inevitably arise, pushing back against the logic of contested settlement and the stories it sponsors. And they emerge not so much out of political resistance as out of spiritual outrage, a conviction that something essentially and preciously human is put in jeopardy by current laws or circumstances. This is how many of us feel when our water and our air and our land are poisoned. We use a spiritual term, a word with deep religious associations, to describe what has happened. We say they have been polluted.

"No Power on Earth—no Magistrate, no Monarch, no Legislature—can oblige me to act against my conscience," said Coleridge two hundred years ago. The voices of objection for many people are spiritual voices, as they were for Coleridge. They are collective voices, cherishing institutions that define their society. And they are bound to particular places, and sometimes to particular languages. This is especially true of aboriginal dissent, and it explains why their conflict provides such a compelling image for a wider range of conflicts between communities, between stories and songs, and between Them and Us.

Liberal-minded individuals often have a bit of a problem with the essential conservatism behind this kind of dissent, and with its determination to protect values that transcend the simple sum of individual preoccupations, values enshrined in the institutions of secular as well as sacred significance in the community, the tribal lore and the tribal law. In the Australian dialect of English, which many Aborigines speak, the words "lore" and "law" sound the same, perfect rhymes in more ways than one.

Also, the stories in which the secular and the sacred are bound together are sometimes hard to believe, like those that say aboriginal people have been here since time immemorial, or that one prophet is truer than another. But prophets don't speak that kind of truth. That's the whole point of prophets; they speak prophecy, which transcends the category of truthtelling without rejecting it. It's the same with aboriginal presence; it deliberately defies a logic of before and after while still insisting on a chronicle of events. We don't need to listen to these stories in a different way; we need to listen to them the same way we do to all stories of a certain sort. Did the Greeks believe in their myths? Yes and no. Were they true? Absolutely.

And yet we need to keep questioning both the authority and the truth of stories, for some of them tell of taking over other people's land, destroying their livelihood, and dismissing their very humanity. We can't just shrug off such stories, for the motives behind them often depend upon the same sense of prophecy, or manifest destiny, or collective mission, that motivates the ones we admire. Here, it is useful to turn to the other side, to the stories that tell of what it feels like to have this done to you. The Aborigines of Australia were telling these stories when I was there, and they were doing so in concert not only with other indigenous people but also with the millions of refugees who have become a fact of life around the world. These refugees have been around for a very long time, although we haven't noticed them until recently. We need to listen to them now. Just in case I have a tin ear, I'll begin with the ones whose music I can understand. And the only way I know how to listen to stories and songs is one at a time.

The outrage of aboriginal refugees in Australia and elsewhere arises out of a conviction that their land has been polluted and their sacred places desecrated, as surely as the statue of the Buddha was destroyed by the Taliban. It has produced a passionate determination to return to the land from which they were evicted, and to protect special places. These sacred sites give meaning and purpose to the Aborigines' world, and they have both symbolic and substantive importance in their lives. They provide a defence against being overwhelmed by reality and isolated from the stories and songs that nourish land and language. Sacred sites offer sanctuary.

There are few topics on which there is such agreement: sacred sites are places of extraordinary importance, from the Buddhist Bodh Gaya to the Shinto shrine at Ise. They can also be places of extraordinary conflict, like the Western Wall and the Dome of the Rock in Jerusalem, usually because of a claim by others that our place is sacred to them too, or because someone has a secular use in mind.

Often, different notions of stewardship bring the secular and the sacred into conflict. In Australia, for example, there are many whites who take a dim view of Aboriginal sanctuary in sacred sites. Legislation leading in the direction of protecting sacred sites is "a symbolic step back to the world of paganism, superstition, fear and darkness," said Hugh Morgan, the director of the powerful Western Mining Corporation. He seemed troubled by the fact that such spiritual attachments were un-Christian. Morgan's Christianity apparently requires that the Crown own the minerals and that people get to work developing them. However much we may dislike what he says, we need to recognize that his reaction has its own spiritual logic. Quoting St. Paul, Morgan insisted that "every man abide in the same calling wherein he was called." In order to do so, the mining industry, like the ranching industry in Australia (until very recently the two largest commercial enterprises), must abide on someone else's land. No worries once again.

Except that people like Morgan *are* worried, for they quite rightly see that their world is changing. And they are responding with apocalyptic anxiety, and a vision of the future that has the whole of Australia eventually falling—or as the Aborigines would say, falling back—into Aboriginal hands; the wheels of progress grinding to a halt; the silence broken only by the whining of didgeridoos and the whimpering of miners and ranchers. Anarchy replacing their hard-won culture.

Lang Hancock, one of the imperial names in Australian mining, put the issue with typical Australian (or maybe Nuu-chah-nulth) candour, again making mining into an almost spiritual quest. "Nothing should be sacred from mining, whether it's your ground, my ground, the blackfellow's ground or anybody else's. So the question of Aboriginal land rights and things of this nature shouldn't exist." As Hancock knows well, in a world ordered especially for mining, maybe nothing *should* get in the way of development but lots of things *do*, things like mountains and deserts and oceans and ice, stubbornly sacred and utterly uncompromising. Aborigines and their claims are facts of life in Australia. Wishing them away will not make them disappear. "The law of evolution says that the nigger shall disappear in the onward progress of the white man," said an Australian politician a hundred years ago. Leaving aside the brutal racism of the statement, there is its retrospective stupidity. Aboriginal people have *not* disappeared, even though there has been no lack of effort on the part of settlers to give God and nature a helping hand.

So now the aborigines in Australia want to do something; but they know they need to say something first. Being constantly asked "What do you really want?" they have come up with an answer. The settlers who came over the past couple of centuries are their tenants, they say. Being responsible landlords, they do not wish to throw them out—they know all too well what that is like—but they do want to negotiate the rent. Including the back rent. Two hundred years' worth.

The slogan "Pay the Rent" had wide currency while I was in Australia. It captured the determination of aborigines to count for something, and to find some ceremonies to settle accounts. A rental agreement would be one. Another, which they also entertain, might be some sort of repatriation to their homelands, or reparation for the holocaust that has overwhelmed them. These are the remedies that have been put forward by people of African descent in the Americas to acknowledge the legacy of slavery, and by Jews to accommodate centuries of abuse culminating in the holocaust of the Second World War.

Even a ceremony of remembrance, some Aborigines suggested, would be a start, since for every jackass who denies the Jewish holocaust there are a hundred who deny what has been done to aboriginal people. Whatever such a ceremony does, it needs to acknowledge the past. In partial response, the Australian Parliament passed a resolution in December 1983 proposing a new basis for reconciliation. Its language was much more straightforward than that which accompanied the Day of Reconciliation—the so-called Sorry Day—in June 2000; and the speech by the Minister for Aboriginal Affairs was even blunter.

The origins of Australia, as the Western nation we know today, are seen by indigenous people here as the end of the Dreaming, not the birth of a nation. For those who had been the custodians of this land for so long it was the beginning of dispossession, disease, and death; in short, of the destruction of Aboriginal society. We expect Aboriginal people to "forget the past and not be bitter" but they do not, of course, because, for them, the past is always present.

Assuming that words were not enough, the government suggested a compact, or maybe a bill of rights. "A bill of rights?" said one Aborigine to another in a cartoon that was circulating at the time. "I thought we paid that one."

And yet words *are* something. Let's look at one set of words. Treaties. They are a traditional way of dealing with apparently intractable disputes and designing new communities of interest. Understanding the principles that informed some of them might help us understand how societies as different as the Greeks and the Persians came to agreement about how to do something more than call each other names or drag each other's dead around in the dust. And how it may sometimes be possible to eat peas with a knife at the same table as my mother and father. Speaking Ukrainian is one way. Signing a treaty is another.

The treaties between settlers and indigenous peoples in the Americas are among the most interesting, for they were attempts to deal with the issues raised by Arnold—the issues of culture and anarchy. Also, they provide a perspective on the long tradition of treaty making around the world. Their original storyline had been made up by the colonial governments, of which the British were among the most energetic in the years of European imperial adventure. The story was then taken over by their successors, including the Americans, until the United States stopped signing treaties with Indians in 1871 because the reservations that had been established under previous treaties had become little more than refugee camps; and, if the truth be told, the army was looking for things to do after the Civil War.

The chief architect of the treaty policy in the English-speaking Americas—the original storyteller, if you will—was William Johnson, who was first appointed an Indian agent in 1744 in what is now New York State, and who established the basic principles that governed British Indian policy for the next hundred years, American policy for a hundred more, and Canadian policy ever since. In fact, for almost a century a member of the Johnson family was in charge of Indian affairs in British North America: on Sir William's death in 1774 he was succeeded by Colonel Guy Johnson, his nephew and son-in-law; and then in 1782, responsibility for the Indian department in British North America was turned over to Sir John Johnson, Sir William's son, who was in charge until he died in 1830. These were the custodians of order, of centralized colonial culture, against the anarchy of what they saw as a dog's breakfast of local arrangements.

Sir William saw good relations with the Indian tribes as a matter of expedience, indeed at times a matter of necessity; and the policy he implemented reflected that view. In a letter to the Earl of Shelburne written in 1767, he described the policy:

Now as the Indians who possess these countries are by numbers considerable, by inclination warlike and by disposition covetous (which last has been increased from the customs in which the French have bred them), I find on all hands that they will never be content without possessing the frontier, unless we settle limits with them, and make it worth their while, and without which should they make peace to-morrow they would break the same the first opportunity. . . .

I know that many mistakes arise here from erroneous accounts formerly made of Indians; they have been represented as calling themselves subjects, although the very word would have startled them, had it been ever pronounced by any interpreter. They desire to be considered as Allies and Friends, and such we may make them at a reasonable expense and thereby occupy our outposts, and carry on a trade in safety.

Johnson knew that any misrepresentation of the Indians as subjects was dubious, not to say dangerous; and although he represented it in self-interested terms, he acknowledged the importance of the process of maintaining alliances and friendships. These were not casual words. They reverberate in eighteenth-century public and private discourse with an implication of interrelated obligations, and an acknowledgment of independent attitudes and ambitions on each side. Different table manners; but table manners nonetheless. Johnson's words also resonate with a sense of mutual interest, of common cause, and of anxieties of the sort that Arnold expressed.

Some thought that the treaties themselves were an indication of anarchy, rather than of a new culture. During the 1830s, the American president Andrew Jackson, fresh from a round of ethnic cleansing in Georgia when the Indian tribes were sent westward as refugees along what became known as the Trail of Tears, said that "treaties with the Indians are an absurdity not to be reconciled with the principles of government." Others, such as the well-informed Lewis Cass, were more resigned to the situation. "The Indians themselves are an anomaly upon the face of the earth," he said, instead of calling them barbarians, "and the relations which have been established between them and the nations of Christendom are equally anomalous. Their interest is regulated out of practical principles."

These were of course the principles of treaty making, which embraced the anomaly of Indian nations just as they now incorporate nations as different in size as Costa Rica and China,

France and Fiji, the United Republic of Tanzania and the United States of America. We seem to have spent the succeeding centuries trying to erase anomalies when it comes to Indian nations, and to entrench them when it comes to the United Nations. But despite a lot of wishful thinking, the native people of the Americas are not going away, any more than the settlers are. Or the Palestinians and the Jews. So maybe there is something to be learned from those who saw the line between self-interest and salvation being best drawn in stories whose contradictions were obvious to all.

There were anxieties aplenty back then, as there are now. The settlers were outnumbered, and often outclassed as well, by the leaders of the tribes, who were men and women of subtle statecraft refined through generations of dealing with other native nations. On the other hand, the native people were outmanoeuvred, at least in the timing of some of the treaties, and they were outsiders to the European ceremonies and texts that became the norm for these negotiations. But they had their own texts and ceremonies, many of which were invoked during treaty making, and they too saw the treaties in terms of a dichotomy between culture and anarchy. They were, after all, not in some hinterland but in their own metropolis, confident in their nationalism and sophisticated in their internationalism. But they were just as aware as the settler societies of the need to find common ground and to articulate a sense of common purpose. Otherwise, nobody would have a place to call home.

There are lessons here that might help us understand situations like those in the Middle East, Eastern Europe and South Asia, which seem more difficult only because they seem more urgent. The history of massacres that preceded, and sometimes followed, the Indian treaties is one that, sadly, is second to none in both ferocity and futility—if not in numbers. For many of us, the denial of humanity with which I began this discussion finds its most compelling contemporary image in the holocausts of slavery and the Shoah, slashed by the genocidal vandalism that has plagued Europe and Asia and Africa for much of the past century. While I would not want to—and could not possibly—discount the absolute uniqueness or diminish the abiding barbarism of each of these experiences and their grotesque heritages, I believe that none of us—white or black or yellow or red—will ever be able to rest in the Americas and call this place home until we acknowledge the brutal campaign, by design and by default, to deny the humanity of aboriginal peoples or, in our more progressive moments, to make them over in our own image. The treaties, for all their faults and failings, remind us that common ground was sometimes found, however briefly, in a sense of civil ceremony.

Despite its British colonial history, Australia had another story-line, a different set of words in which treaties didn't figure and there was less opportunity for shared belief. In *The Cake Man*, a play by the black Australian writer Robert J. Merritt, there is a scene in which an Aboriginal man (called Sweet William by his affectionate wife and not so affectionate son) turns in surprise to discover the audience. "Uh, how you?" he says. Then, grinning craftily, "Hey, you wanna buy a boomerang?" The boomerang, it turns out, is made in Japan, and the Australian champion boomerang thrower is a white fellow. Sweet William, on the other hand, is "a Kuri, the Australian Aborigine, that's who I am and what I am . . . made in England."

Merritt's play was inspired by the situation of his people, the Wiradjuri, and their wretched circumstances at the Erambie Aboriginal Mission Station in Cowra in New South Wales where he grew up. But even within that wretchedness there remained a sense of hope and possibility, mixed of mem-ory and desire and an unconquerable faith that overrode the black humour by means of which people maintained a measure of sanity in a world that no longer made sense. At the end of the play, Sweet William is musing—drunkenly—on the old question: "What is it that aborigines want?"

Forget all that shit about giving me back my culture. That's shit. It isn't what I'm really after, not really. What I want, what I'm here for is . . . it's something else again, if I could get across what I mean . . .

[*Pause. He sits down*]

Look, I'll tell you something. No laughing, you're not allowed to laugh but you gotta try to listen and not call me a liar or laugh. I'm no liar . . . ask Rube, ask my missus, she'll tell you that's one thing about me, that I ain't a liar . . . one thing I'm not . . .

[*Pause*]

You ever heared of a eurie-woman? You say it like that, eurie-[*you-ree*] woman. No? Never heared of one a them? Well listen, then, I'll tell you what's a eurie-woman, and what it is I want here.

I was working at Killara Station . . . after I had me feed, I went an' laid down on me bed an' started readin' this gubba [white man's] book I had . . . [*Wide-eyed*] . . . an' all of a sudden I heared this emu drummin' somewhere close, I got up an' wen' outside an' stoked up the fire, an' all the time this emu was still drummin'. I's tryin' to hear 'zactly where it was so I could find that nest . . . then the drummin' started closer to the tent. I was just sorta curious, like y'know?

[*Pause*]

I thought I won't have no trouble findin' that nest in the morning . . . but this time it was right behind the tent.

[*Pauses dramatically*]

Sooooo . . . while I was turnin' 'round I got the biggest fright of me whole fuckin' life! It weren't no emu, it was a woman. And she had hair that was shinin' black, an' it hung right down over her backside. She was the prettiest woman I ever saw . . . yeah . . . she was a eurie-woman . . . I fair bolted out a there! You'd a thought I had wings, the way I flew out a there . . . [*shaking his head slowly*] didn' do me no good . . . must have run easy a mile . . . but just as I ducked through the fence wires, there she was again, right in front of a man . . . between me an' the road . . . an' it was summer hot as fuckin' hell but I had this freezin' cold sweat all over me . . . an' then I took off again, runnin' for me life, scairter than ever I was before, runnin' fast . . . but didn't matter how or where, she was always there in front of me, and at the same distance away from me . . . her hair shinin' and swirling like it was made out of water, an' her skin like black lightnin', if y'can imagine that . . . so beautiful she couldn' ever be bad . . . but she was scary anyway, an' always there in front of me . . . but somewhere else.

[*He pauses, in reverie*]

Well, all I remember then is a gubba I was workin' for was sayin' to me what was wrong what happened . . . an' I said didn't he see that eurie-woman . . . an' just the way he looked at me I knew he never had, that he never would or never could see that eurie-woman . . . a gubba. Ain't no eurie-woman for gubbas, she came to tell me so I'd know.

[*Pause*]

[*Smiling*] Y'know what? He said: "Come on William, ain't no eurie-woman . . . come back to reality."

[*Pause*]

[*Smiling sadly*] Exac'ly what that eurie-woman was sayin' to me . . .

[*Pause*]

Two realities.

[*Pause*]

An' I've lost one.

[*Pause*]

But I want it back . . . I need it back.
[*Pause*]
Not yours . . . mine.

For Sweet William, reality is the imagined ideal, the dream vision, the eurie-woman. She doesn't "represent" anything, doesn't imitate anything; she just is. A contradiction in terms. She is his answer to the riddles of life—"who are you?" and "what are you doing here?" All the other things—the so-called realities of his life, its despair and degradation—are phantasms, spectres, shadows. And those shadows—the mimicry and mockery that make up his sense of himself—are killing him as surely as any poison.

One would think that we would be more comfortable with dreams like Sweet William's. After all, twentieth-century psychology has been all but obsessed with the reality of dreams. But perhaps we are not as far ahead as we think in negotiating the border between reality and the imagination.

One of the people I met in Australia was Geoff Clark, whose Aboriginal home was in the southern Australian state of Victoria, near the damp and cloudy maritime climate that takes some of its sharp edge from the Antarctic. His people had managed recently to get some of their land in trust, after a hundred years of exploitation by the Board for the Protection of Aborigines, which had been set up in 1860 in the State of Victoria. Whatever the board was protecting, it certainly was not land. In 1957, only 4586 acres remained out of the millions that had once been Aboriginal homelands in the region.

The struggle of Clark's people centred around a forest. It was a place where the spirits were abroad. I grew up surrounded by trees, the cedars and firs of the northwest coast of North America, and I almost always feel at home in the woods. But this forest was a brooding and restless place, a place where for the first time I recognized the unease of spirit that Aborigines had been talking about to me since I had arrived, a place where the dead were being disturbed. The Aborigines there had finally persuaded the state government to recognize their authority. But first they had to blockade the road through the forest.

Blockades are interesting, whether they're to stop the building of a dam or against Cuba and Iraq. They say, "Don't come over the border," not so much to keep people out—though of course they always have that ambition—but to signal that there *is* a border. They function like the threshold of a church, or the beginning of a story; and they need to be acknowledged if proper respect is to be paid to those for whom the place is sacred or appropriate contempt shown to those who are polluting it. The nineteenth-century cleric John Henry Newman wrote a book called *The Grammar of Assent*, in which he talked about how we come to say "yes" to faith. The grammar of aboriginal hopes and fears, the logic that informs their stories and songs, is a spiritual grammar; it is not a social or economic or political or even a cultural one. It is grounded in a knowledge and belief in something beyond easy understanding, expressed in the stories and songs as well as the dances and paintings that speak about the spirits. And it pushes back against both the pressure of reality and the rhetoric of other people's imaginations. It is a blockade too, saying no to other ways of being in the world.

Blockades establish borders; and border conflict appears in various contexts: between the useless and the useful, as we have seen; between farmers and hunters; and between dreamers and doers. Sometimes it takes still other forms. One is the clash between the human and the non-human—as old as the hills, I suspect—which reappeared during the encounter between settlers and aboriginal peoples. It is still with us in the awkward arguments over abortion, euthanasia and cloning that we are all trying to avoid but where the true sense of the word "human" gets a very strenuous workout. Another border conflict is between human beings—especially their arts and inventions—and the natural world. I love rivers and mountains and birds and bears, and I am not fond of the roads and dams that break them up and destroy their habitat. But like the Shakers, I also love chairs made of wood, and I love songs that have words, which bird songs generally don't. Sometimes this conflict generates one of those choices that are suspiciously like those I said are impossible.

I faced such a choice many years ago. The story begins high in the Rockies where there's a town—more like a curve in the road—called Canal Flats. It's hard to find on the map, harder still to recognize when you get there, having asked directions from the north, say, following the river (and the Shuswap Indians) up through Death Rapids to the dry benchlands and the low-lying marshes where the glacial waters of Finley Creek and the hot springs of Fairmont come together on the flats at the headwaters of the Columbia; or, coming from the south, following the Kootenay River (and the Kootenai Indians) up from Montana, past the flats to the headwaters high in the sawtooth mountains of the Rocky Mountain trench. These two great rivers pass within a hundred feet of each other, going in different directions, at Canal Flats, where years ago they dug a canal to join the river systems. The rivers won, and an old sternwheeler now sits lodged in the mud, a testament to human arrogance.

The Columbia runs north in Canada to a place called Boat Encampment, at the head of what we used to call the Big Bend, and then sweeps south through the northwest United States 1200 miles to the sea. The Kootenay heads south to the United States, passing by the rolling country and rodeo towns of Montana and Idaho, where it turns north again to Canada and the lake country of the west Kootenays. I spent much of my youth there, and I grew up on these rivers, running the length of the Kootenay several times by canoe, and once—once was enough—along the dangerous Big Bend. I came away with a powerful sense not only of this natural heritage but of the ways in which it has shaped the lives of those who lived within it.

It is sometimes said that we should think of God as a verb, not a noun. For me, these rivers were pure verb, infinite power. There have always been folks who want to turn them into nouns, or finite resources. Maybe naming rivers is our first mistake, our original sin.

In any case, this grammatical disagreement led to my first real venture in civil disobedience in the early sixties. A blockade. Along with many others—most of them unlikely protesters from the railroad town of Revelstoke—I tried to get arrested by lying down in front of the bulldozers that were about to begin work on the Mica Creek dam, the first in what would eventually become a large hydroelectric project (rivalling those lower down the Columbia), stretching from High Arrow to Kinbasket Lake and flooding some of the greatest wilderness areas in the Northwest. It was accompanied by the Libby Dam and other smaller projects on the Kootenay, backing the waters up into the valley of the Purcell Mountains. We didn't get thrown in jail; they simply walked the cats around us. And of course we didn't stop the dams. But we did talk a lot about how, in Henry David Thoreau's words, "in wildness is the preservation of the world."

A couple of years later, living in Vancouver, I went to hear the great folksinging group the Weavers, with Lee Hays, Ronnie Gilbert, Eric Darling and Pete Seeger. To me, their songs represented all that was progressive and promising about the world, and they embodied the possibilities of resistance in our actions and revolution in our attitudes. I wouldn't have missed them for the world. Then Lee Hays led off with Woody Guthrie's classic "Roll On, Columbia"—and I didn't know whether to laugh or cry.

Now Guthrie's song, which was set to the tune of Leadbelly's classic "Goodnight Irene," was one of twenty-six that he wrote under the sponsorship of the Department of the

Interior and the Bonneville Power Authority. He had come to the Northwest out of the dust bowl and the Depression, with a deep sense of the plight of the dislocated and the dispossessed. And he believed that since institutions were the major agents of dispossession and dislocation, institutions (especially those generated by government initiatives) should provide the main remedy. So he promoted the hydroelectric projects of the Bonneville Power Authority, whose dominant image at the time was the Grand Coulee Dam. He wrote a song about that too, set to the tune of "The Wabash Cannonball." Indeed, his description of both the Grand Coulee Dam and the Columbia River has something of that railroad song's wide-eyed wonder. Here are a few verses from "The Grand Coulee Dam."

> Well, the world has seven wonders that the travelers always
>   tell,
> Some gardens and some towers, I guess you know them
>   well.
> But now the greatest wonder in Uncle Sam's fair land,
> It's the King Columbia River and the big Grand Coulee
>   Dam. . . .
>
> She winds down the granite canyon and the bends across
>   the lea,
> Like a prancing, dancing stallion down her seaway to the
>   sea;
> Cast your eyes upon the biggest thing yet built by human
>   hands,
> On the King Columbia River, it's the big Grand Coulee
>   Dam.
>
> In the misty crystal glitter of that wild and windward spray,
> Men have fought the pounding waters and have met a
>   watery grave.

Yes, it tore their boats to splinters, but it gave men dreams
    to dream,
Of the day that Coulee Dam would cross that wild and
    wasted stream. . . .

Uncle Sam took up the challenge in the year of 'thirty-three,
For the farmer and the factory and for all of you and me.
He said, "Roll along, Columbia, you can ramble to the sea,
But river, while you're rambling, you can do some work
    for me."

It doesn't take a literary critic to recognize the insignia of naturalness and wild dominion, each of them associated with the river; and of ingenuity and industry, identified with the government and the dams and developments they sponsor. The power of the Columbia, mighty and majestic, is not so much controlled as it is harnessed, the way one might harness horses or oxen—which become, like the river, no less themselves for being made useful to humans. In this image, the Columbia becomes a useful river, like the Nile; but it remains a great river, also like the Nile. It is a modern river; but it is one that somehow retains the ancient aura of the wilderness— a frontier wilderness that had been announced closed by the United States Census Bureau in 1890 but which remained wide open in the American imagination. In this region of the imagination, the river is both wild and civilized, both a part of nature and a part of us. There is a powerful iconographic tradition that comes into play here too, where some rivers—like the Columbia—have a larger than life status. Mountains and oceans sometimes share this, and so does the weather. Though all of these can be harnessed to human use, they remain ultimately beyond our control, and therefore beyond our caprice. Not exactly useless but wild, almost barbaric in their antagonism to civilized order.

Therein lies their importance; and if we lose this, some would argue, we have lost much, including the ability to do something other than lie down in front of a bulldozer. "As long as the rivers flow," goes the promise of many of the Indian treaties, perhaps in some measure out of a cynical conviction that flowing rivers are among the few things likely to last longer than the next administration, but, more profoundly, signalling a belief that where other sanctions (such as those of the Bible) are not shared, this provides one of the few rhetorical gestures that brings together a sense of natural and supernatural authority. Stop the rivers, goes the underlying logic, and something unthinkable will happen, because something both unnatural and unholy has been done. The projects that Guthrie celebrated stopped the Columbia River, and in doing so both literally and figuratively polluted the land.

But they also did something else, and this is where the conflict comes in. They held promise of controlling the drought and the flood, those twin scourges of the settled world and yet also part of that same overwhelmingly natural world. They were manifestations of one of the venerable parables of agricultural settlement: turning a wasteland—sometimes construed as a wilderness—into a garden; making the desert bloom. There is a powerful Judeo-Christian rhetoric at work here, in which the land that brings forth plenty is deemed to be blessed by God, while the land that does not is cursed. One of the markers of divine disfavour is the barren land. In Islam, too, which like Judaism is originally a religion of the desert, the waterhole is a blessed place. And after all is said and done, nobody, not even the Aborigines of Australia, can do without water forever.

So things get very complicated. The Aborigines might say that Guthrie sang in the waterholes, celebrating the dams that would, in words from "Roll On, Columbia," "run the great factories and water the land" of the Northwest so that "rich farms would come from the hot desert sand." Guthrie sang (in his words) "at all sorts and sizes of meetings where people bought bonds to bring the power lines over the fields and hills to their own little places. Electricity to milk the cows, kiss the maid, shoe the old mare, light up the saloon, the chili joint window, the schools and churches along the way." He sang a praise song to the people, and to hydroelectric projects that, once again in the words of "Roll On, Columbia," would "turn the darkness to dawn" and give hope and possibility to children and their parents. They would turn the majestic into the manageable, the useless into the useful.

From the Arctic National Wildlife Refuge to the rain forests of the Amazon we are struggling with contradictions here. What is the place of the wild, and of wilderness, in our world? How can we balance the need for useful development with the necessity to preserve sanctuaries of almost defiant uselessness? And what exactly is this thing that we call the wilderness anyway? Much of our unease about the barbaric and the civilized, and about Them and Us, has to do with our uncertainty about this distinction; and about its corollary, the place of human beings in the natural world. As the American writer Gary Holthaus says:

> We talk of the "natural world" as if there were another, unnatural world. We talk of "sacred places" as if there were other, non-sacred places. We talk of getting back to nature, as if we could possibly ever tear ourselves away. But there is no other place, there is only this one entirely natural world, and the trashed out back alley sitting in the shadows of concrete is as sacred as the mountain top, and as natural. The styrofoam cups in the bar pit along the road, and the corner behind the dumpster, covered with vomit from one of our culture's homeless drunks, is also natural, and therefore sacred. The red rock arches of the West may be more

pleasing, but no more sacred, less changed by human
endeavour or human failure, but no more natural.

We may not go as far as Holthaus, but there is wisdom in
his reminder that we cannot choose between the sacred and the
natural, any more than we can between the real and the imagined, or between being isolated and being overwhelmed. And
many of the conflicts we have been talking about—over livelihood and language and land, for example—are as much about
the sacred and the profane as they are about the civilized and the
barbaric, or the useful and the useless. Ironically, it may be at
sacred sites like the Temple Mount/Haram esh-Sharif in
Jerusalem where these conflicts will be both renewed and resolved.

At the end of the day, it is the place we call home, a place
with both sacred and secular significance, that provides our
most reliable point of reference for understanding these conflicts, whether in liberation movements seeking to establish a
homeland or in the various stories of exile and the experience
of diaspora with which we are regaled almost every day.

PART II ⁊ *Losing*

It

FOUR

There's No Place Like Home

"Lost, unhappy and at home." That is how the Irish poet Seamus Heaney felt when he visited an ancient burial site in Denmark. The bodies, remarkably well preserved in the peat bog and showing clear signs of ritual sacrifice, reminded him of his native Northern Ireland and the violence that was tearing it apart.

It is the feeling of many people haunted by home. My father's favourite phrase was "There's no place like home." Loving the play of language, he taught me that if we just take that little word "like" away, what we are saying is "Home is no place." Nowhere. And yet, of course, what we also mean is that home is right here, a good place, the ideal place. Utopia. Then it really *is* nowhere, for that's what "u-topia" means: no place.

Home. Here and nowhere. Or maybe it is elsewhere. The poet Philip Larkin has a poem titled "The Importance of Elsewhere"; written in Ireland, it is about his home in England. Certainly home is caught up in contradictions between reality and the imagination, here and elsewhere, history and hope. Many of us, from time to time, have probably felt lost and unhappy at home. For adolescents, that's what families are all about. As we get older, we might agree with Ishmael in Herman Melville's novel *Moby Dick* when he describes the home of the strange harpooner Queequeg. "It is not down in any map," he says. "True places never are." A Mexican ballad that once had currency right up through the Southwest told of a place whose streets were paved with precious metals, its wells filled with olive oil, and its churches made of sugar. It was called "City of I Don't Know Where."

This, of course, is also the place of stories, the place where things happen that don't and things are that are not. One of the stories that catches this contradiction as well as any is to be found in Rastafari and its musical expression in reggae, in which the Biblical story of Jewish exile and return is made over into the African experience of slavery in the Americas. "By the rivers of Babylon we sat down and wept," sang the Old Testament psalmist, lamenting a loss beyond language and assuring the spirits back home that, "If we forget thee, O Jerusalem, our tongues will cling to the roofs of our mouths."

"They that carried us away captive required of us a song. . . . How shall we sing the Lord's song in a strange land?" asks the singer. We cannot, he implies, but then he goes right ahead and does so, singing a song that is still giving solace both to the Jewish people of the world for whom the legendary King David is an ancestor and whose sufferings never seem to be over, and to those Africans brought as slaves into exile in the Americas, for whom The Melodians—the Jamaican rocksteady singing group which preceded reggae —provided what the psalm refers to as "a melody in their heaviness." Their song "By the Rivers of Babylon" has become the anthem of Rastafari.

Songs like this don't really bring the dead back, or take you home, do they? Oh, but they do; they surely do. Maybe a good place to begin is with this contradiction and what is possibly the most difficult challenge we face these days. It has to do with the unspeakable evil that haunts every one of us whether we realize it or not—the holocaust of the Second World War and the holocaust of slavery. And another, closer to many of us than we might realize—the unremittent horror that has characterized relations between native peoples and newcomers in the Americas, Australia and Africa, as well as parts of Asia.

How can we find some consolation, some sense of ceremony, in our contemplation of these stories?

For a start, we need to recognize that there is a connection between them. Rastafarianism has acknowledged this connection most clearly. Born of Babylonian exile and a reading of Biblical prophecy that identified the late Emperor Haile Selassie of Ethiopia (whose name before his coronation was Ras Tafari) as the black Messiah, Rastafarianism has become one of the great myths of the Americas, with its account of wandering and exile and its dedication to the idea of home. It has given comfort to people from all walks of life, if only through the extraordinary popularity of reggae. And it has forged a connection among these three stories of horror, identifying the Americas as a place not only of African dislocation but also of the dispossession of the aboriginal peoples of the land, and it has linked both to the archetypal experience of Jewish exile and slavery described in the psalms. We *all* know, each in our own way and according to our own beliefs, that "if we forget thee, O Jerusalem, our tongues will cling to the roofs of our mouths." This Jerusalem is both an original home and a future one, and I believe it is in this very uncertainty, and only in it, that we can find a way through the conflict of Them and Us to a place we can all call home.

The Barbadian scholar and poet Kamau Brathwaite poses the question for all of us, whatever our colour or creed. "Where then is the nigger's home," he asks, "in Paris, Brixton, Kingston, Rome? Here, or in heaven?" Home may be in another time and place, and yet it holds us in its power here and now. Home is like our language, compelling us to think and feel in certain ways and giving us the freedom to imagine other ways and other places. It is who we are and where we belong. Home both binds us and liberates us. Home is the tapestry that Penelope was weaving and unweaving as she tricked her suitors and waited for Odysseus; it was both his winding sheet and his welcome, whichever was required. It is Persephone, shuttling between her husband, Hades, and her mother, Demeter, winter and summer, the underworld and the everyday world. It is Charlie Tjungurrayi, talking about *tulku* and *tjukurrpa* to someone who doesn't know the words but understands the meaning. It is not anybody's exclusive Jerusalem, neither Arab nor Jew nor Rastafarian nor Presbyterian, nor even the Jerusalem of William Blake's great hymn. It is a meaningless sign linked to a meaningless sound out of which we each build the shape and meaning of our lives.

What Rastafarians have done is to make up a story—and I say this in high tribute—that will bring them back home while they wait for reality to catch up with their imaginations. It is an immensely powerful story, and its influence through the music of reggae is a measure of that power and a reminder that we do not need to share the legacy of slavery in order to understand the longing for home that is central to the experience of Rastafarians, and of so many Africans living around the world. Or of Jews hoping to meet in Jerusalem next year. Or of Palestinians living in refugee camps on land their parents once called their own. Or of aboriginal peoples around the world, homeless in their homeland. Rasta and reggae provide a ceremony of consolation and commonality even as they present a litany of suffering. They provide one example of the way beyond conflict and loss—through the very stories and songs that remind us of them. The other way, of course, is to forget. History, as the great nineteenth-century French historian Ernest Renan once said, specializes in forgetting.

In many ways, home is an image for the power of stories. With both, we need to live in them if they are to take hold, and we need to stand back from them if we are to understand their power. But we do need them; when we don't have them, we become filled with a deep sorrow. That's if we're lucky. If we're unlucky, we go mad.

For the fact is that stories keep us sane and steady in a world in which we are always having to face loss and unhappiness. Death presents us with the most drastic of these experiences, which is why elegies and laments and funerals and memorials are among our most important ceremonies of belief, and why—in one of the greatest of all contradictions—they often make us feel better.

Home—the idea as well as the reality—has something of the same power; and one of the things we will turn to later is a set of stories about home that have given people the strength to go on, and often (sadly, for the world) the determination to fight on. But for now, I want to look at the situation of those who have no home, or who are haunted by homelessness, or who are just plain homesick.

Until we recognize how the sorrows and sufferings in one culture can help us understand another, we have little hope of finding a ceremony of belief that we can share, one that will counter the chronicle of public events that plagues us all. It is a chronicle that includes much of what has gone on for thousands of years in communities from Asia and Africa to Europe and the Americas. The sad fact is that the history of settlement around the world is a history of displacing other people from their lands, of discounting their livelihoods and destroying their languages. Put differently, the history of many of the world's conflicts is a history of dismissing a different belief or different behaviour as unbelief or misbehaviour, and of discrediting those who believe or behave differently as infidels or savages. The first three chapters of this book were about the dynamics of this dismissal; the next two are about its devastating consequences, in this case the loss of home.

Homelessness haunts us all. One of the reasons we walk so nervously around the homeless on our streets is that we don't want to get too close to something we fear so deeply. The derelict man in the ditch or the doorway is one version. Another is the story of dislocation and dispossession, of exile, of being without a haven here below or in heaven above, which we have already glimpsed from time to time in this book. It has a very powerful hold on our imaginations, and gives to places like the Middle East their bewildering character, seemingly beyond the logic of compromise or the rhetoric of consolation.

For the moment I want to turn back to the Aborigines of Australia. Despite all the clichés about their nomadic existence, these wanderers have home at the centre of their lives. That is why the loss of it has been so traumatic. Here is the anthropologist W. E. H. Stanner talking about how "no English words are good enough to give a sense of the links between an aboriginal group and its homeland."

> Our word "home," warm and suggestive though it be, does not match the aboriginal word that may mean "camp," "hearth," "country," "everlasting home," "totem place," "life source," "spirit center," and much else all in one. Our word "land" is too spare and meagre. We can scarcely use it except with economic overtones unless we happen to be poets. The aboriginal would speak of "earth" and use the word in a richly symbolic way to mean his "shoulder" or his "side." I have seen an aboriginal embrace the earth he walked on. To put our words "home" and "land" together into "homeland" is a little better but not much. A different tradition leaves us tongueless and earless towards this other world of meaning and significance. When we took what we call "land" we took what to them meant hearth, home, the source and locus of life, and everlastingness of spirit. At the same time it left each local band bereft of an essential constant that made their plan and code of living intelligible. Particular pieces of territory, each a homeland, formed part of a set of constants without which no affiliation of any

person, no link in the whole network of relationships, no part of the complex structure of social groups any longer had all its coordinates.

Stanner described the consequences as "a kind of vertigo in living."

> They had no stable base of life; every personal affiliation was lamed; every group structure was put out of kilter; no social network had a point of fixture left. There was no more terrible part of our . . . story than the herding together of broken tribes, under authority and yoked by new regulations, into settlements and institutions as substitute homes. The word "vertigo" is of course metaphor, but I do not think it misleading. In New Guinea some of the cargocultists used to speak of "head-he-go-round-men" and "belly-don't-know-men." They were referring to a kind of spinning nausea into which they were flung by a world which seemed to have gone off its bearings. I think that something like that may well have affected many of the homeless aborigines.

This feeling affected many of the Aborigines from whom Chatwin got his inspiration, and it affects many people around the world today. Unless we understand this, and acknowledge the *idea* as well as the reality of the homelessness that afflicts us, it is going to be difficult to understand the conflicts that are shattering our world.

One of the problems, as I have suggested, is that home is so difficult to place, both literally and figuratively. As with many other things that we hold dear—justice, clean air, quality education—we are better at describing what it is not than what it is. That's why every story about home is like the U2 song "I Still Haven't Found What I'm Looking For." A prayer.

Perhaps Homer's story of *The Odyssey* has such perennial appeal because it is a story of a homecoming, even though it takes ten years for it to happen; and because it has a happy ending, unless you were one of Odysseus's companions (all of whom die before they reach home) or one of his unwelcome guests (all of whom he kills). It is a story about the doubts and distractions of a homesick man, finished with Troy but fighting warlords and weather as he heads home to his wife. His story is fabulous, telling of strange adventures and heroic feats outside the realm of possibility, but it is also familiar.

Odysseus wasn't perfect, not by a long shot. He was a seagoing salesman with a gadget for every purpose and a girl in every port. He was a con man and a crook, with a violent temper and a wide streak of self-pity. His troubles weren't entirely his fault, of course; some of the gods, a lot of the people, and most of the monsters he meets are not very friendly. Much of his story, in fact, is about what it is like to be a stranger.

We all know something of what it feels like to be a stranger from the experience of being elsewhere, whether we went there by career choice (Odysseus was a warrior, off to work) or in chains. But it is, I suggest, something different to be a stranger in your own home. Odysseus tried it briefly, going into disguise when he first got back to Ithaca; then in order to reclaim his home he went on a murderous binge that would make a Mau Mau or a Palestinian freedom fighter—both terrorists, if you are on the other side of those conflicts—look like wimps. Aboriginal people around the world will tell you they feel like strangers in the languages they now speak, in the livelihoods they have been forced to take up, in the literatures they are given to read. Many have turned back to their own languages and literatures to find ways of recovering the idea of home, and to tell their tales. Sometimes this has been in court, where they try to convince others. Often it is within their communities, as they recall traditional stories and take themselves back home, even as many of them remain homeless.

The Viennese call a person who looks after a house a *hausbesorger,* which literally means a "house-worrier." People around the world know what it is to "worry for their country"; the phrase is a common one among those who have left their homeland to live elsewhere. They feel a responsibility not so much on behalf of the present generation as for those who have gone before and those who will come after. The Aborigines of Australia talk about "growing up the country" the way a parent would talk about bringing up a child, for they know the land grows and changes. But in their case they also know that the land is still in their custody. They live with the knowledge of what is around them, and with the memory of those who have gone before in a past that extends far back to the "dreamtime," when their ancestors created the places and the names by which they know the land and pursue their livelihood as hunters and gatherers. According to their beliefs, the country and its people were originally created by spirits, who made the rivers, the water holes, the hills and the rocks and all the living things. They gave each clan its land and its dreamings: stories and songs about the animals in whose form the spirits dwell. The dreamings are also about the responsibility of the Aborigines to these spirits, who return to the earth at particular places which are now sources of power as well as part of the landscape. Their descendants, the Aboriginal men and women now living there, are the custodians of this power, and of the land. They hold the keys to the kingdom, and the secrets of the temple. *Tulku* and *tjukurrpa*.

But the Australian Aborigines are also like many other people around the world, dreaming of home even as they live in a kind of schizophrenic limbo, like Sweet William, or in the vertigo described by W.E.H. Stanner, displaying all the insignia of homelessness.

The homelessness of Mitch Gregory, whom I sat beside during a flight across north Queensland to the small community of Kowanyama on the Gulf of Carpentaria. He was a broken-down rodeo cowboy, returning home. He had smashed his arm and shoulder in the local rodeo a month earlier and had been in Cairns for medical treatment. His mind was on the next rodeo, and whether he'd be ready; but from the moment we flew over the mountains and first caught sight of the Mitchell River that ran down to the coast, he began to speak of "my country," his Aboriginal homeland. He told of boar-hunting trips, and rounding up brumbies, as wild horses are called there; and he talked about the use of some of the area by the community to graze its own cattle herd, which provided much of their meat during the "big wet," the half of the year that they are isolated from all road traffic by the heavy tropical rains. His sister was chair of the Kowanyama Community Council but Mitch was not particularly interested in politics, which had been difficult under the pressures of a state government that wanted (after a century of brutal disruption) to turn the community into a showplace. A decade ago, they had no control at all over their own lands, or their lives; they were reduced to one water tap for each tribe, daily rations and a set of chores that included sweeping the steps and whitewashing the stones leading up to the government administration building.

As we talked, Mitch kept returning again and again to his country, that part of the Mitchell River over which his people once had full authority, some of which they were now trying to regain with the two other tribes they had been forced to live with in Kowanyama. They had applied for powers under a new self-management act; and although nothing happened for a while, the Queensland government had eventually promised a deed of trust to the community, covering at least a small part of the territory that had been their domain. The idea alone made Mitch Gregory feel that the river whose name he bore, and whose banks he knew like the back of his smashed up hand, was really going to be his again after all. When we arrived on the small landing strip at Kowanyama, I was met by the government administrator rather than one of the Aboriginal leaders. As we got off the plane and Mitch saw the man, his confidence collapsed and he was once again a nobody, living nowhere. Mitch, tamer of horses, might as well have been dragged around the walls of his home town. Many people will recognize something of Mitch Gregory in their own lives.

For homelessness is also a condition of mind and spirit. It is the gut-wrenching emptiness described by Robert Service in one of the Yukon ballads that my father used to recite.

> Out of the night, which was fifty below,
> and into the din and glare,
> There stumbled a miner fresh from the creeks,
> dog-dirty, and loaded for bear.
> He looked like a man with a foot in the grave
> and scarcely the strength of a louse,
> Yet he tilted a poke of dust on the bar,
> and he called for drinks on the house.
>
> His eyes went rubbering round the room,
> and he seemed in a kind of daze,
> Till at last that old piano fell
> in the way of his wandering gaze.
> The rag-time boy was having a drink;
> there was no one else on the stool,
> So the stranger stumbles across the room,
> and flops down there like a fool.
> In a buckskin shirt that was glazed with dirt
> he sat, and I saw him sway;
> Then he clutched the keys with his talon hand—
> my God! but that man could play.

Were you ever out in the Great Alone,
    when the moon was awful clear,
And the icy mountains hemmed you in
    with a silence you most could *hear;*
With only the howl of a timber wolf,
    and you camped there in the cold,
A half-dead thing in a stark, dead world,
    clean mad for the muck called gold;
While high overhead, green, yellow and red,
    the North Lights swept in bars?—
Then you've a hunch what the music meant . . .
    hunger and night and the stars.

And hunger not of the belly kind,
    that's banished with bacons and beans,
But the gnawing hunger of lonely men
    for a home and all that it means.

And homelessness is a farm auction. Those who have been to one will know the scene: the family there in the background, leaden-hearted, watching while their past is laid out for everyone to pick over, knowing that their future depends on how much they pick up during the next two or three hours. The men try not to cry, but few succeed; the women, who are stronger, try not to bid on a favourite item—something bought thirty years ago when the youngest child was born, or twenty years ago when a sister died, or ten years ago when the old man stopped drinking, or five years ago when the first grandchild came along. They are hoping against hope that their neighbours will find a way to pay more than they can afford for livestock and equipment they don't really need, and which they look on as partly their own anyway since they have helped raise and repair them. Meanwhile, the auctioneer shows all the tricks of his trade, humouring the friendly vultures circling about the yard with lighthearted comments about the bits and pieces of a lifetime of laughter and tears, and trying to sell things that are both priceless and worthless.

We may not all know such emptiness, and I hope we never do. But I suspect we all know what it is to be homesick, even if it is not on the scale of the descendants of African slaves or wandering Jews or the indigenous peoples of the world who have lost their land through various forms of thievery and trickery. We know their stories and songs; and in any case, all our literatures are filled with images of homesickness. There is a moment in one of the great poems in the English language, John Keats's "Ode to a Nightingale," that catches the feeling. Keats is moving from a celebration of the immortal song of the nightingale to a particular instance.

> The voice I hear this passing night was heard
> In ancient days by emperor and clown:
> Perhaps the self-same song that found a path
> Through the sad heart of Ruth, when, sick for home,
> She stood in tears amid the alien corn.

The passage owes its effectiveness partly to the noble story it tells from the Old Testament of the stranger in Judah, working in the fields of grain. But it is the honesty of the phrase "sick for home" that transforms the sorrow into something other than a set piece, catching the anguish of being human, and being homesick.

There are many images of this home, in many cultures, and they are all, like William Butler Yeats's lake isle of Innisfree, "heard in the deep heart's core." We find them in the story of Odysseus, "heartsick on the open sea, fighting to save his life and bring his comrades home." And in descriptions of the home Calypso offers him when she proposes to make him immortal. The home of the gods is

> never rocked by galewinds, never drenched by rains,
> nor do the drifting snows assail it, no, the clear air
> stretches away without a cloud, and a great radiance
> plays across that world.

This is the home we all long for, the Jerusalem we are not to forget. It may be the place we came from, five or fifty or five hundred years ago, or the place we are going to when our time is done. It is the place we still haven't found but are looking for. The place that gives us a sense of our self, and of others.

But figuring this place out turns out to be a problem for many of us. It is a problem for me. I don't come from anywhere, except the Americas. And somebody else calls this place home, somebody who isn't always happy having me around. Even here, my family has always been on the go, moving on with so many other families in North America. I have three photographs of my grandfather: in one, he is sitting on a Red River cart, heading west from Regina to Fort Macleod in southern Alberta in the early 1880s; in another, he is standing on a log boom, painting his boat, a sturdy old northwest-coast runner, in the 1930s; and in the third, he is sitting in the backyard of our house in Vancouver in the 1940s, holding me in his lap and telling me the story of how one day he left to go travelling . . .

"We live our lives as a tale that is told," says Psalm 90, the funeral psalm. But before the funeral, we would like to get the story right. So in the spirit of Merle Haggard's country-and-western song "Sing Me Back Home Before I Die," here are a couple of my attempts, both of them more or less made up.

The first goes like this. I was born close by the rain forest, and for a while we lived in a little cottage owned by one of the woodsmen, right under the bridge that spanned the entrance to the harbour we called Lion's Gate. Later, I went to the interior where my relatives lived and got to know the desert lands between the mountains, and the savannahs beyond. Great rivers ran through this country, one of them over a thousand miles long, its watershed covering more than a quarter of a million square miles, with rapids and waterfalls rivalling any in the world, and the flow of water twice that of the Nile. When my grandfather first went there, very few travellers had been through before, though Amerindian peoples had lived there for millennia.

There had been slavery in the place where I grew up, and there were people who remembered that grim story: how the slaves and indentured labourers harvested the rich resources of the land, while its wealth was accumulated by a small elite. But for all its wretchedness, the society was rich in artistic creativity, with dancing and drumming and carving and painting and beadwork and basketry of exquisite craft and design. So important was dancing, in fact, that when the colonial government passed a law banning it, the people responded with stubborn independence. A strict law bids us dance, they said, in words that became an anthem of resistance for many of my generation.

There was a lot of trade in the region, both along the coast and into the interior; and many of the stories and songs I first learned were about either fascinating old trade routes or the mysterious bonds of kinship. Politics played its part in all this, further fractured by class and ideology: basically, those working the land formed one group, and their managers and overseers another. Every time one group came into power, some of the others would end up in jail. Criminalizing the opposition was a local custom. There was a political party that believed that everyone, artists as well as farmers, should be given credit for their contribution to society. It wanted us to print our own currency.

There were places of refuge, maroon fastnesses where runaways nurtured their distrust of their enemies and worked on their dislike of each other. Some came from far away across the waters to hide out in the mountains and valleys, shaping societies that were locked in time as much as they were held in place.

The languages people spoke varied widely, with English taking on a homemade inflection that was routinely mocked by our colonial schoolmasters. There was a pidgin language that had developed out of the coastal trade, and some of its words found their way into the lexicon of standard English and onto the map as place names. And there was another language, which we would probably now call a creole. I used to hear it occasionally around the house, for the spiritual guide assigned to me when I was born spoke it. And there were still other languages brought there by people who came looking for gold, or sent by God.

I recall listening to one community singing psalms in a language I had never heard before, and seldom since. Because they had been persecuted throughout much of their history, and for over three centuries had been on the run over continents and oceans, they had coded their own experiences and beliefs into these psalms. They sang them not only in their strange language but in a style designed to make them unintelligible to almost anybody else, the words being drawn out over a succession of musical phrases that were further extended by the staggered breathing of the chorus to produce a continuous sound and little interpretable sense. "The singing of psalms is like honey," began one of them. It took over five minutes to sing those seven words, syllable by syllable.

In secular as well as sacred ceremonies, oral traditions were a central part of my world. Teaching was mostly memorization; political gatherings were arenas of dramatic oral performance; and laws had to be read out before they came into effect. Most religious practices involved a mix of spoken and written texts and of old and new rituals, though many maintained that their particular practices were drawn from a pure source, of distant but (at least in the minds of the custodians) distinct memory. And everyone prayed in several places and forms, inhaling everything from exotic incense to local opiates, and from the finely pulverized wood of the rain forest to the salt sea air. We were hedging our bets, to be sure; but this was also part of our search for a ceremony of belief that could give meaning and value to our lives, and to the land.

This was where I was born. It will sound to my friends and family unfamiliar, for I have described it in language usually reserved for other places, where other folks live. It wasn't the central highlands of Brazil or the coastal mountains of Chile, nor was it any part of Guyana or the Amerindian strongholds of Central America. It was, as you will know by now, the northwest coast and mountainous interior of Canada. Looking at a map of the Americas in 1858, Queen Victoria had added the word "British" to distinguish it from the Caribbean Colombia, with which it shared much both geographically and demographically. So British Columbia it was called (though its founding father, James Douglas, was of African as well as Scottish heritage).

My other story is less exotic, and is the one I live in every day. Next to it, the first one looks made up. But of course both are. The rain forest was temperate, but it *was* an overwhelming presence in our lives; the Amerindians were Kwakwaka'wakw and Tlingit and Nuu-chah-nulth and Nisga'a, all of whom had slaves well into the nineteenth century. The pidgin language was Chinook, which I mentioned earlier; and Michif was the creole language, born over three hundred years ago of contact between French, Cree and Ojibway traders, and further enriched by other encounters. Linguists continue to argue about it, calling it variously a pidgin, a creole or a dialect of Cree. My godmother—the spiritual guide I referred to, who also taught me card tricks and told me contradictory creation stories—spoke Michif; but she was of the generation who thought it nothing more than a slang, spoken by half-breeds like herself.

The political party was called Social Credit; though they liked bankers better than socialists, and were always at odds with the workers. The psalm singers were Doukhobors; their name, originally derogatory, means "spirit wrestlers." They were refugees from religious persecution in Russia who had come to British Columbia around the turn of the century and retreated into the mountains, the most radical calling themselves Freedomites and reading the Bible as an exile's covenant. Even more sternly than Rastafarians, they rejected any compromise with Babylon, burning houses and possessions (including occasionally all of their clothes) in acts of ritual purification. They also refused to send their children to school; and so the authorities sent in the police to take the children away, and then they built a special jail, hundreds of miles beyond the mountains, for some of the more belligerent parents who had turned to occasional acts of violence. *Terror in the Name of God* was the all too familiar-sounding title of a book written about them in the early 1960s. Soon the rest of the community, many of them very old and most of them women, walked all the way down to the coast to sing their psalms outside the walls of the prison where their fathers and husbands and sons were being held. They used to say that when they stopped singing psalms in that way, they would stop being a people.

Stories like this have to do with belief; and belief involves a conflict between the true and the untrue. But it also requires that we forgo a choice between them. One would think that Joseph Campbell and all the New Age advocates would have brought us to a greater understanding of this, and of the ways in which the experience of living our life as a tale that is told is shared. But they have not. One reason may be that we have not recognized how such stories and songs work, and how it is in contradiction that they bring comfort, not obliterating the feelings of loss and longing but rather reminding us of them even as they release us from their hold. This paradox is central to their power. "I am a man of constant sorrow," says the strangely comforting song.

FIVE

Gaelic Is Dead

I REMEMBER SOME YEARS AGO watching, on television, the Ayatollah Khalkhali parading the corpses of dead American soldiers in Tehran, soldiers who had come on a hapless mission to rescue hostages being held by Iran. It was a barbaric scene, and those who saw themselves on the side of the hostages felt helpless and afraid.

I should probably have used another word than "barbaric" to describe the scene. It is not for nothing that people refer to the "theatre of war," for this was unmistakably theatre, staged to appeal to the aesthetic as well as the ethical sensibilities of its audience—and to deeply offend them. It was also war, of course, when death stalked the ramparts; the spectre behind the ceremonies. It was barbaric too, frighteningly so, not because the Iranians were barbarians but because their leaders wanted to behave like ones, putting themselves deliberately beyond the pale of civilization. Or maybe they were setting one kind of theatre, the theatre of desecration, up against the theatre of a decent burial.

The word "barbarian," as I mentioned earlier, was first used by the Greeks to describe the Persians (whose home included the land that is now Iran), because they didn't speak Greek. Defying the need for ceremony, as the ayatollah did, was an ironic signal of its importance to him, even as it confirmed his understanding that it was important to us. He might have had in mind the occasion in which it was the *Greeks* who behaved like barbarians, when Achilles dragged the body of Hector in the dust around the walls of the city until finally, on the command of Zeus (and on payment of a large ransom, much like that paid by the Americans for their soldiers), Achilles delivered up the body for a proper burial.

"Thus held they funeral for Hector, tamer of horses." The promise of those final words might even help us two thousand years later, whether watching the terrible events in Tehran or the latest product of our contemporary theatre of terror.

But stories don't *really* help, do they? "The classics can console. But not enough," wrote the West Indian poet Derek Walcott in a poem about the travels of Odysseus after the fall of Troy and the funeral of Hector. To expect comfort from a bunch of words "is like telling mourners around the graveside about resurrection. They want the dead back," he added elsewhere.

Behind this impossibility is the old choice between reality and the imagination. Typically, it presents itself to us with an urgency we cannot ignore, even—or perhaps especially—when we recognize that it is not really a choice at all. Although we may feel hopelessly caught between death and resurrection, somewhere in us we know that the cold grip of winter will eventually give way to the warm flow of spring, that no matter how overwhelming our grief or how intense our sorrow it will eventually give way to grace, if only the grace of numbness or exhaustion.

Hector's story surely helps. But it does so first of all by reminding us of the very thing we are trying to forget—the despair, the hopelessness, the experience of being frozen in anger and incomprehension. Some of the world's greatest stories do exactly this: two others that come to mind are Dante's *Inferno*, which begins with the poet lost in the dark woods, desolate and afraid; and the Greek myth of Demeter, whose daughter Persephone was taken from her by Hades, the king of the underworld, and whom she searches for in vain until finally in her grief she brings upon the earth a year of famine. But

Hector has his funeral; the Roman storyteller Virgil appears to Dante and leads him through hell to the hope of heaven; and Zeus sends his messenger, Hermes, to persuade Hades to let Persephone return every spring, bringing joy and renewal.

Every tradition has a version of this storyline, reminding us that for millennia other people just like us, all around the world, have felt as Rachel did in the Old Testament book of Jeremiah; she "weeps for her children and does not want to be consoled, because they are not." There is no condition more terrible than this, and yet there also seems to be an abiding faith, across time and in different places, that there *is* some consolation for such sorrow in ceremonies of remembrance.

All of us are acquainted with grief. Such grief is usually private and personal. But there is another grief that overwhelms us from time to time, a very public grief, bringing with it a different kind of anguish and a no less debilitating despair. It is more than the loss of home itself, it is the loss of everything that makes us human. It is the loss at the heart of the story of Hector being dragged in the dust around Troy by the victorious Achilles, and the ayatollah parading the bodies of dead American soldiers in Tehran. In one sense, their atrocity is inseparable from all conflict such as war, which fosters the categories of barbarian and civilian in order to both perpetuate the antagonism and prolong the misunderstanding. But there is something more going on here. "Atrocity," writes the Canadian poet Don McKay in "Fates Worse Than Death," "implies an audience of gods."

> The gods watched as swiftfooted
> godlike Achilles cut the tendons of both feet
> and pulled a strap of oxhide through
> so that he could drag the body of Hektor,
> tamer of horses, head down in the dust
> behind his chariot. . . . Atrocity

is never senseless. No, atrocity is dead ones
locked in sense, forbidden
to return to dust, but scribbled in it.

"Dead ones locked in sense, forbidden to return to dust, but scribbled in it." It is not only the war dead that haunt us. It is also the Aborigines of Australia and the Indians of the Americas and the Bushmen of the Kalahari who are paraded about, just like the body of Hector, in museums and monographs around the world. And the Africans murdered on the Middle Passage and in the swamps and savannahs and sugar-cane fields of the Americas. They are all unburied, suffering a fate worse than death and haunting us with the incompleteness of their lives.

"When the Highlands loses its language, will there be a Highlands? . . . In what language would you say *'Fhuair a'Ghaidhlig bas,'* "Gaelic is dead'?" asks the Scots poet Iain Crichton Smith.

If the classics cannot console, how can *any* ceremony, *any* words or images, be adequate to commemorate the death of a language, the death of a people, the death of a friend? That question—which could be the psalmist's, asking "How can we sing the Lord's song in a strange land?"—is at the heart of the power of stories. It is also the beginning of reimagining Them and Us in order to find common ground in a world of conflict.

Let's go back for a moment to Odysseus, suffering

many pains . . . heartsick on the open sea,
fighting to save his life and bring his comrades home . . .
his heart set on his wife and his return.

Wandering the world, Odysseus was a man of many sorrows, losing hope as the years went by, looking for love in all the wrong places, watching all his comrades die, heartsick and homesick—a sad man travelling among scary people and places. His story is told by Homer with extraordinary pulp-fiction violence, but many aspects make it relevant to our everyday lives. James Joyce took it up and turned it into his novel *Ulysses*—Odysseus's name in Latin—about an unremarkable day in Dublin; and many others have tried their hand at making it new. It is a sorrowful tale of mischief and mischance, and yet people seem to feel happy hearing about it. Strange.

Recently the Coen brothers made Odysseus's story into a movie called *O Brother, Where Art Thou?*—its title taken from a throwaway line in a 1940s comedy by Preston Sturgess, *Sullivan's Travels*—with a signature song beginning, "I am a man of constant sorrow." It is an old southern lament, most famously sung by the great country singer Ralph Stanley, and it tells about Odysseus in Appalachia.

I am a man of constant sorrow,
I've seen trouble all my days;
I bid farewell to old Kentucky,
The place where I was born and raised.

For six long years I've been in trouble.
No pleasure here on earth I found,
For in this world I'm bound to ramble,
I have no friends to help me now.

It's fare you well, my own true lover,
I never expect to see you again;
For I'm bound to ride that northern railroad,
Perhaps I'll die upon this train.

You may bury me in some deep valley
For many years where I may lay,

Then you may learn to love another
While I am sleeping in my grave.

Maybe your friends think I'm just a stranger,
My face you never will see no more,
But there is one promise that is given,
I'll meet you on God's golden shore.

It is certainly not a cheerful song, with its litany of trials and tribulations. It does hold out a kind of consolation, but as Derek Walcott would probably say, not enough. And yet a lot of people who take no comfort from the promise of heaven have received a great deal of comfort from this song. Most of us will never know the extravagant distress described there. But we all know something of the melancholy that begins *Moby Dick,* when Ishmael says, "Whenever I find myself growing grim about the mouth; whenever it is a damp, drizzly November in my soul; whenever I find myself involuntarily pausing before coffin warehouses and bringing up the rear of every funeral I meet . . . then I account it high time to get to sea as soon as I can."

"The truest of all men was the Man of Sorrows," Ishmael says later, and we nod our heads knowingly. Some of us may even recognize Dante, sunk in deep depression at the beginning of the *Inferno,* describing

How hard it is to tell what it was like,
this wood of wilderness, savage and stubborn
(the thought of it brings back all my old fears).

At such moments, life certainly doesn't bring many smiles. But stories and songs about it seem to.

During the 1930s and 1940s, when people were losing their farms and their families and were trying to hold on to almost anything, they listened to the radio. And the songs that made them happy were often very, very sad songs. "I Am a Man of Constant Sorrow" was one. (For those who are wondering where the women were, there was another version written by Sara Ogan, a young miner's wife in Harlan County, Kentucky, who had to leave her home because her family was blacklisted from the mines for taking part in a strike. It was called "Girl of Constant Sorrow.")

And then there was Jimmie Rodgers, dying of tuberculosis and singing his "T.B. Blues," one of hundreds of blues songs in black and white that caught the imagination first of southern folks and then of all of us. It used to be said that during the Depression the typical shopping list for a southern farm family was a pound of butter, a slab of bacon, a sack of flour and a new Jimmie Rodgers record.

> When it rained down sorrow,
> It rained all over me. . . .
> I'm fighting like a lion,
> Looks like I'm going to lose
> 'Cause there ain't nobody
> Ever whipped the T.B. Blues.

Or maybe it was Hank Williams they were listening to, singing on the Grand Ole Opry and all over the Americas:

> Hear that lonesome whippoorwill,
> He sounds too blue to fly.
> The midnight train is whining low,
> I'm so lonesome I could cry. . .

> Did you ever see a robin weep
> When leaves begin to die?
> That means he's lost the will to live.
> I'm so lonesome I could cry.

All of these songs are from one tradition, down country, but there are versions everywhere. They pick you up on your way down. They put you back together by telling what it's like to be broken apart. They make you feel better by making you feel bad. They give you Charlie Chaplin, making "a grail of laughter of an empty ash can" (in the words of American poet Hart Crane); or Homer Simpson, whose sad-sack life makes my son Geoff howl with laughter and (so he insists) provides him with lessons for a happy life.

And they give us something beyond laughter and tears. Billie Holliday, for example, singing "Good Morning Heartache."

> Good morning heartache, here we go again.
> Good morning heartache, you're the one who knew me
>   when . . .
>
> Might as well get used to you hanging around,
> Good morning heartache, sit down.

Or Huddie Ledbetter (Leadbelly), with his great ballad "Goodnight Irene."

> Sometimes I live in the country.
> Sometimes I live in town.
> Sometimes I take a great notion,
> To jump into the river and drown.

Let's look at one song that may be less well known these days, called "When the Work's All Done This Fall." It was written in the 1890s and recorded in 1924 by Carl Sprague for RCA, when it sold a million copies. The song tells of a cowboy who, after a lifetime of riding the range, announces that at the end of this season he is going back home to Dixie with what's left of his wages . . . instead of doing what he would usually do, which is spend it all on drinking, dancing and some other unmentionable activities.

The song turns around images of home: his broken-hearted mother's home, which we know cannot be quite the same place he left long years ago, but to which he plans to return after this last round-up; his home on the range, one that has held him for so long; and his final home, which he refers to (in a familiar figure of speech) as the "new range" to which he will soon be called by his master.

It also turns around another notion, one that is not stated in so many words but rather in so few rhymes. Let me try to explain. The chorus of the song goes like this:

> After the round-ups are over and after the shipping is done,
> I am going right straight home, boys, ere all my money is
>   gone.
> I have changed my ways, boys, no more will I fall;
> And I am going home, boys, when the work's all done this
>   fall.

The night after he announces this, the cowboy is out riding herd when a storm comes up. The cattle stampede; he tries to head them off; his horse stumbles in the dark, falls on him, and he is fatally injured. The final verse of the song tells the words that are carved on the wooden board that marks his grave:

> Charlie died at daybreak, he died from a fall
> And he'll not see his mother when the work's all done this
>   fall.

Now one of the things that I remember thinking first about this song was that the fellow who wrote it must have been pretty short on rhymes. Both in the chorus and in the final verse he rhymes "fall" and "fall"—a sure thing, I know, but embarrassingly simple-minded.

Yet there's method in this monotony, for he makes us immediately aware of the several meanings of "fall" that he is using. In the chorus, "fall" refers both to the season—a season of harvest, of the round-up and shipping of cattle—and to the sinner who has fallen from grace. (As the first verse has it, "I am an old cow-puncher and here I'm dressed in rags./I used to be a tough one and go on great big jags.") The final verse presents another pair: his fall from the horse, and the season again, but this time it's a season of death, of another kind of round-up. As a result, the song resonates with both ripeness and regret, conveyed in the various meanings of "fall"—figurative and literal, literary and local, secular and sacred. William Wordsworth once remarked that we are fostered both by beauty and by fear. Fall figures in both, and "When the Work's All Done This Fall" uses the season both to commemorate a death and to find consolation for it.

Finding consolation requires ceremony. In 1876, Truganini died. She was the last of the Aboriginal Tasmanians in what is now Australia, and her life was a chronicle of the depredations that had been inflicted upon her people, and upon her family. Her sister had been stolen, her mother stabbed, her husband mutilated and left to drown. She had been kept in a certain sort of comfort in her last years, but she was haunted by fear, a fear that others would steal her body and mutilate her corpse. "Don't let them cut me up," she pleaded as she died. "Bury me behind the mountains," from where she could see the beach where her husband had died and the place where her people belonged. But they put her in the prison cemetery instead.

A hundred years later, Truganini got her last wish. But much evil had been done in the meantime, and her people are now determined to put the ghosts of their dead to rest. They have no doubt that the classics can console, but they also know they need classics from their own traditions, an audience of their own gods bearing witness to the atrocities that have been inflicted upon them and watching over them as they bury their dead. Without this, even if the reality of their lives changes for the better, they will continue to be overwhelmed by someone else's ghosts, or someone else's gods, coming from the great water rather than the wide desert. Aborigines in Australia, and refugees everywhere, want to complete the unfinished business of Truganini.

The poet Patrick Lane tells a story from British Columbia that catches another aspect of this experience of living with the dishonoured dead. It was a time when progress meant roads and hydroelectric dams and the obliteration of Indian villages and of Indian gravesites . . . or all but a few, for the tourists.

> The cracked cedar bunkhouse
> hangs behind me like a grey pueblo
> in the sundown where I sit
> to carve an elephant
> from a hunk of brown soap
> for the Indian boy who lives
> in the village a mile back in the bush.
>
> The alcoholic truck-driver
> and the cat-skinner sit beside me
> with their eyes closed
> all of us waiting out the last hours
> until we go back on the grade
>
> and I try to forget the forever
> clank clank clank
> across the grade

pounding stones and earth to powder
for hours in mosquito darkness
of the endless cold mountain night.

The elephant takes form—
my knife caresses smooth soap
scaling off curls of brown
which the boy saves to take home
to his mother in the village

Finished, I hand the carving to him
and he looks at the image of the great
beast for a long time
then sets it on dry cedar
and looks up at me:
     What's an elephant?
he asks
so I tell him of the elephants
and their jungles. The story
of the elephant graveyard
which no one has ever found
and how the silent
animals of the rain forest
go away to die somewhere
in the limberlost of distances
and he smiles

tells me of his father's
graveyard where his people have been
buried for years. So far back
no one remembers when it started
and I ask him where the graveyard is
and he tells me it is gone
now where no one will ever find it

buried under the grade of the new
highway.

This image passed through my mind as I stood in a small
Aboriginal camp just north of Alice Springs in central Australia
in 1984; and now, nearly twenty years later, it represents the
condition of so many people around the world, especially those
living as refugees in their homeland. There is no Palestinian
child, I suspect, who would not recognize this story as his or
her own . . . just as there is no Jewish child who will not have
been told a story just like this.

I was visiting in Australia with a group of Aboriginal men
and women from across the country who had gathered to discuss what to do about their homelands, haunted by restless
spirits. They talked about many things, but in the evening, after
a day of dealing with details, they talked about their ancestors,
some of whom were resting uneasily as museum exhibits or
skeleton curiosities in the hands of the Australian anthropologists. Other ancestors had been lost from sight, and many had
died alone and unremembered. The land where their spirits
remained had fallen into other hands, and the spirits wandered
about. So, in a sense, did many of their descendants, those with
whom I was sharing a meal around cooking fires set in old oil
drums, with open fires for conversation under a clear and surprisingly cold desert sky.

There on that mid-winter night in June, the conversation
was about breaking free, and not just from the past. It was
about breaking free from stories and songs which, like their
land, had been taken over by someone else, and which denied
their ceremonies as surely as any ayatollah ever did. This was
a gathering of the Federation of Land Councils, a group of
state and territorial organizations that had played an important
part over the previous decades in getting some land back into
Aboriginal hands. The land councils marked a new beginning

for Aborigines in Australia, but not yet the end of their heritage of sorrow and suffering. Patrick Dodson, one of the most widely respected Aboriginal leaders of that time, talked about the routing of a new railway line up to Darwin, in the Northern Territory. Like the lines of the nineteenth-century British surveyors who mapped out and renamed much of the British Empire, the railway menaced a spiritual legacy that linked places according to a logic much more rooted in the landscape and in the lives of the Aboriginal people than road grades and steel rails, but much less obvious to European settlers.

Dodson and some of the others around the fires had worked out an arrangement whereby the general regions where the spirits dwelt would be identified by the Aborigines without locating the specific sacred sites, and the railway would avoid these areas. They would be closed, and the ceremonies could then coexist with the settlers.

The spiritual logic of Aboriginal peoples in Australia, the logic that determines both their attachment to the land and their obligations to it—their grammar of assent, as Newman would have put it—is not designed to persuade those outside the community. It is like their languages, of which it is a part. Those inside the languages or the community are bound by it; and those outside may not even notice. Dodson and others are trying to translate; but like all translation, it is not always successful and is sometimes scorned by the community itself.

Still, there are other strategies for those in exile by the rivers of Babylon. Geoffrey James, another of the Aborigines around those nighttime fires, had come to the meeting from his small settlement way out in the Gibson Desert. Several years ago, he led a few others along what is known as the Canning stock route to a place that had been their ancestors' home. "Settle down country" was the phrase he used. Life for his people was difficult there, but it was better than life in the towns. And it was home. His presence at the gathering was, like

Dodson's, something special. Both of them, in ways that I slowly realized, were setting their people free. Free to be in one place and never to wander again. Free to be house-worriers at home, where the spirits are.

This next story has to do with a language and a people that are having even more difficulty holding on. It is a story of loss of life, of language and of land, and of almost unspeakable suffering. But like those songs of sorrow, it is a story that may help us all.

I first met them living in a scrap wood and sheet metal house on the edge of a ragged township scattered around a rocky outcrop called Swartkop, about two hundred miles from the southern edge of the Kalahari Desert. Driving by, it looked like a garbage dump . . . which in a way I guess it was. There were three sisters and their cousin: |Una, Kais, |Abakas and Griet. They were ≠Khomani, a small group of so-called Bushmen, and the language they spoke was strange even to the linguist who was with me. ("|" and "≠" represent two of its five click sounds.)

The ≠Khomani had once been a relatively large group— large for a hunter-gather society, at least—living in the surprisingly rich desert and semi-arid lands that make up the west central highlands of what is now South Africa, north of Cape Town. The flourishing culture that had been theirs, and the relatively affluent life they led, were reminders that it might have been the cradle of human life, where culture and craft and science and the arts began.

The old name for the Bushmen was the San. After thousands of years as hunters and gatherers, they had themselves been hunted down and gathered up, essentially as slave labour, by the herders and farmers who came into their homeland. First there were the migrations of Bantu-speaking people from the north, hundreds of years ago; then came the European settlers who found what was left of the San and their strange looks and even stranger-sounding languages. With their bows and poison arrows they were not a welcome sight to the settlers, who thought of them as vermin and sought to clear them out by any means possible. The story of the San Bushmen is one of the grimmest stories in the history of the last millennium, a holocaust whose numbers may not match those of the Nazi regime or the slave trade or the murderous campaigns against aboriginal people in Australia and the Americas, but whose horrors rival them all.

Somehow, some of them survived. During the mid-1990s, one of the leaders of the ≠Khomani, Petrus Vaalbooi, led a small group of Bushmen in the development of a land claim to recover their homeland. They were encouraged in their claim by the new African National Congress government, which had been elected in 1994 and was committed to the redistribution of land following the collapse of apartheid. Having written eleven official languages into its new constitution—none of them indigenous, partly because nobody thought there were many indigenous people left in South Africa and partly because nobody much cared—the government was determined to demonstrate the aboriginal presence in the country in any way it could. Restoring at least part of the homeland of the San people of the Northern Cape was a start.

Up until then, the few who claimed Bushman heritage were known mostly through the grotesque caricatures that accompanied historical accounts of the region, or because of the exotic touch they added to the tourist trade, wearing skins and making bows and arrows and necklaces to sell to tourists. David Kruiper, a traditional leader who worked alongside Petrus Vaalbooi, was one of these; he had lived with his extended family for a time in a private game reserve in the Karoo (south of the Kalahari) called Kagga Kamma, where tourists could come and meet "authentic" Bushmen. Another hunter who became part of the campaign to recover land and language was Jakob Milgas, whom I first met

wearing skins and selling necklaces to tourists by the side of the
dirt and gravel road about two miles from the entrance to the
Kalahari Gemsbok National Park (now called the Kgalagati
National Park). Each time a car went by, he and his family were
completely enveloped in dust. Meanwhile his elegant photo-
graph, showing him in skins against a backdrop of red Kalahari
sand, graced the postcards you could buy just down the road in
the gift shop at the entrance to the park.

It is an old story. The South African novelist Nadine Gordimer
told me that in 1936, when she was a child, she went to the
Johannesburg world fair (called the Empire Exhibition). There
she saw on display some Bushmen from the Kalahari, several the
same age as her. They were in fact these same sisters |Una and
Kais and |Abakas, who were first taken from the desert in the 1930s
to be put on show by the ayatollahs of southern Africa. They
weren't quite dead yet; but the assumption was that they, and their
people, soon would be. They are "one of the most primitive people
of the world, whose extinction, if a reserve is not created, can
scarcely be prevented," read a caption in one newspaper.

The ANC government was as good as its word (perhaps
encouraged by the fact that Nelson Mandela's ancestry, recorded
in his face, is partly San). Within a couple of years, and in the
face of considerable opposition from farmers and herders in
the region, it had settled the claim, an action that should put to
shame countries like Canada and the United States, where land
claims have often languished in the courts and Congress for
generations while Indians languished on reserves. A good part
of the territory they once called home and knew by heart was
restored to the ≠Khomani, with substantial allocations of land
(much of it purchased by the government from the current
landowners and leaseholders), special access to the park (now
jointly managed by South Africa and Botswana) for the collection of medicinal plants, and financial resources. The struggle
is not over; but the San are back in their homeland.

The success of any aboriginal land claim depends on a detailed demonstration of use and occupancy of the territory, usually back beyond the time when written records were kept. During the process in the Kalahari, the land claims lawyers who were working with the ≠Khomani knew that being able to identify places and events in their ancient language would be very helpful . . . but of course that wasn't possible since the language was no longer spoken. Or so they thought. One of them said nostalgically to Petrus, "It's too bad nobody still speaks the language." "*Ma praat hom,*" he replied, in the dialect of Afrikaans that he speaks. "Mum does."

Elsie Vaalbooi was the mother of the mother tongue. She was ninety-seven (in 1998), living in a township called Rietfontein on the Namibian border, and so it was there that a group went to pay their respects and to determine whether the language she spoke was in fact the original language of the ≠Khomani. It had all the family resemblances that linguists look for, and it did indeed seem to be the language transcribed by conscientious collectors of endangered species in the late nineteenth century, albeit in that inevitably imprecise way of any script as it tries to represent sounds, especially from a language with a variety of clicks and tones unfamiliar to other European languages or Arabic, the other widely dispersed written script of Africa. It had been assumed that the Bushmen's way of life was doomed along with their languages, like the languages and livelihoods of the vanishing North American Indians. By the middle of the twentieth century, the language of the ≠Khomani had been pronounced dead.

But it wasn't. Not quite. Elsie Vaalbooi thought she was the only one left alive who spoke it—Petrus, her son, certainly didn't, nor did his children—and she expected that it would soon die with her. But in a gesture of faith she spoke into a tape recorder, sending a message to anyone who could hear. Fortunately her faith was not misplaced, and so far about thirty more speakers have been found by following up on rumours about someone who spoke funny, or looked funny, or knew the old ways, or could find their way in the desert. There may be a couple of dozen more scattered around the Northern Cape. None of the ones we know are young. Many have been living alone, or with no other speakers around. Now they are gathering together in settlements that have taken shape as part of the land claim agreement.

I was with │Una Rooi and Kais Brau and │Abakas Koper and Griet Bott on their first return to their aboriginal homeland in the desert. We visited a site near the park entrance where there was a stone marker to commemorate "The Last of the Bushmen," the wistful or wishful thinking of an earlier generation, and probably also an attempt to provide a funeral ceremony of sorts for the San. But now here they were, in ages from four to seventy-four—Petrus and David and Jakob and his young son were with us—the last of the last of the Bushmen . . . and the first of the returning San. Their epitaph, as Mark Twain would have said, was an exaggeration.

Though maybe not much of one. When │Una stood on the dune and spoke her language, she turned the occasion into a ceremony of belief as compelling as any funeral. As I write this, only she and Kais are still alive. Griet died of cancer; │Abakas of heart failure following a lifetime of living with the tuberculosis that is endemic in their community these days. Others are following fast.

Still, the ≠Khomani have begun to speak out in their own language about their history and their home. I watched the old women stand on the red sand and take back the land, mapping out a precise geography of the imagination in stories and songs, while the men deciphered and disputed over tracks in the sand with the delight of scholars who have been let back into the library after being shut out for decades. They stood under a tree down behind a large dune, one of only about a

half-dozen trees as far as the eye could see, and told about how
| Una had broken that branch when she was a youngster, sixty
years ago, and where Kais had jumped off the dune. I had been
driving all day, with fourteen of us in a van built for seven,
through desert that looked pretty indistinguishable to me, and
I must admit that I was wondering to myself whether this was
really the same tree. Just then the sisters, standing on top of
the dune, spoke about how they remembered the tree because
the sun went down right over there at this time of the year—
and they pointed across the street (as the valleys between the
dunes are sometimes called) to where the sun's rays slanted
across the sand. At almost the same moment one of the hunters
dug up an old stone at the base of the tree, covered with ash
from a cooking fire, and another found a shard of pottery.
And the sisters told how they had served tea in a cup made
from that same piece of pottery to a collector-entrepreneur
named Donald Bain, who had come to take them to
Johannesburg and put them on show; and how on their return
they found their houses had been destoyed. On a visit to the
local magistrate, their father asked, "Where do you expect us
to go?" "Who do you think you are, speaking to me that
way?" replied the magistrate angrily, and kicked their father in
the stomach so hard they thought he might die—which he did
not long afterwards.

On the wall of my room as I write this I have a picture of
an Indian woman, Mrs. Jimmy, whose son I used to hunt with
in the Rockies. She is in a hospital bed, smoking a cigarette with
a fierce intensity, the last native speaker of her Kootenai dialect
in that part of the country. She died three days after the photo-
graph was taken. In a gift of grace, the language has been taken
up by the next generation, who have learned it from those who
speak it as a second language.

Something the same is happening with the language of the
≠Khomani. It is from the family of Khoisan languages and is

called N|u, though that name is more a convenience than any-
thing else. When I asked the sisters what they called their language, they looked at me with the pity people reserve for the
really stupid. "We don't have a name for it," they said. "We
just speak it." N|u means "to speak."

Led by Levi Namaseb, a gifted linguist and storyteller from
the University of Namibia, the ≠Khomani are recovering their
language. Namaseb has developed a new orthography for N|u,
and is teaching both the youngsters and the older generations.
They have the sounds, for most of them speak Khoekhoe, a
related language; and they have the interest, for now that they are
back in the desert they want to learn about it through the names
of its plants and animals and spirits and stars. But around them
hovers the ≠Khomani version of the question Iain Crichton
Smith asked about Highland Gaelic. In what language would you
say, *"Ng xanki ≠khoake |'aa"; "*N|u is dead"?

Language is a perennial contradiction. It is supposed to nourish
communication, and yet often it does just the opposite. It is supposed to sustain communities, but often it breaks them apart.
Some of the Bushmen hunters whom I went with into the
desert—Petrus and David and Jakob, for example—are extraor-
dinarily skilled hunters, legendary in the land. They are at home
in the desert. But they have lost their language and do not speak
N|u. Does this make them second-class Bushmen, less ≠Khomani
than those who do? If N|u is the language of their homeland and
they cannot speak it, will they ever really be home? This question bothers them, I know. It also divides the community.

Beyond that there are other questions. Does speaking in
Gitksan or N|u or Hebrew or Gaelic enhance the authority of a
story, or of a storyteller? Do we live our lives as a tale that is
told in Yiddish or Yoruba or Estonian or English? If so, which,
and why, and how? The answers are important for a number of
reasons, among them the influence they might have on our

efforts to ensure the continued life of a language. If what is important about a story is simply its plot and its characters and its theme and all the other interesting stuff that we learn in the classroom or from Joseph Campbell, then why not just write it down and translate it? Why is it necessary for Mary Johnson or | Una to sing their songs in their languages, except to make them—and maybe us—feel better? On the other side of the coin, how does the Qu'ran speak to contemporary readers? How does Shakespeare; or the Bible? Is it in the untranslatability, or perhaps just the unordinariness, of texts that the genuine common ground lies?

I want to end with a story about another death, one for which words did come easily. It was first told in medieval Europe and then retold by Alfred Tennyson in the middle of the nineteenth century, about the death of the legendary King Arthur. It is about a war, and loss, and how consolation and comfort come with the proper ceremony. It is also about the relationship between public and private grief, and how stories and songs can make that distinction disappear.

> So all day long the noise of battle rolled
> Among the mountains by the winter sea;
> Until King Arthur's table, man by man,
> Had fallen in Lyonnesse about their Lord,
> King Arthur: then, because his wound was deep,
> The bold Sir Bedivere uplifted him,
> Sir Bedivere, the last of all his knights,
> And bore him to a chapel nigh the field,
> A broken chancel with a broken cross,
> That stood on a dark strait of barren land.
> On one side lay the ocean, and on one
> Lay a great water, and the moon was full.

This is about a king who has fallen in battle and now is dying. The scene is filled with sorrow, and yet somehow, in a strange way, it conveys joy . . . a contradiction of emotions we experience in everything from Shakespearean tragedies to sad songs. It is not just that we know that Arthur, like a good mythical fellow, won't really die. The scene also brings to us some of the deeper contradictions that lie at the heart of human existence.

It does so by setting up dramatic contrasts, moving from the wonderfully infinite to the pitifully finite and back to the infinite again, much as we all do when we contemplate life and death. Images of limitless expanse frame the picture, from the noise of battle rolling all day long around the mountains by the winter sea, to a dark strait of barren land surrounded by the ocean on one side, and on the other a great water, with the full moon overhead. At the centre, isolated in the middle of these awesome images, is the simple figure of Arthur, whose wretchedness is mirrored in the pathetic chapel, with its broken chancel and broken cross, and in the friendship of his last surviving knight who bears him there. His mortal injury is almost casually introduced, with a matter-of-factness that contradicts the melodrama of the scene.

"Then, because his wound was deep." Suddenly, and only for a moment, the legendary king becomes human, becomes mortal. It is a moment of human clarity and of limitation. It is also a moment of mystery, and limitlessness. It is a moment that has analogues in every tradition of stories and songs, and when we have learned it in one, we can recognize it in another. It is the moment that every ceremony tries to recreate, and it contains within it a contradiction that seems to have a permanent hold on us.

In what language would you say, *"Fhuair a'Ghaidhlig bas,"* "Gaelic is dead"? In a language of contradictions, strange and familiar all at the same time.

PART III ❧   *Reality*

and the Imagination

SIX

To Be or Not to Be

WHEN I WAS A CHILD I would check under the bed every night; and then in the closet, looking carefully behind the clothes. There was a box in the corner that got a kind of strip search, and a small space behind my bookshelf that needed a flashlight. And then after all this I would look again under my bed before I got in, just in case one had sneaked over there behind my back. Ghostbusting was hard work. And even with all that security the ghosts slipped out of my sight and into my dreams. There they were like the great water and the full moon, filling me with wonder.

As Wordsworth said, wonder is nourished by both beauty and fear. It was fear that I felt going to bed. I remember a little prayer I used to say as a child—and indeed long after, when I thought it rather silly. It was my insurance.

> Now I lay me down to sleep,
> I pray the Lord my soul to keep.
> If I should die before I wake,
> I pray the Lord my soul to take.

The sentiment is pretty simple; and part of its simplicity—which is also part of its initial appeal—arises from the way in which the rhythms and rhymes reinforce each other. "Sleep" and "keep" pull together in one direction, "wake" and "take" in another, in almost perfect time. But then we begin to hear other things that take a deeper hold on us. Sleep is a place of safekeeping, the rhyme suggests, and yet we're talking about dying; indeed, if that weren't a possibility we wouldn't be saying the prayer. So the rhyme takes this up and generates new contradictions: "sleep" suggests the loss of consciousness, but it rhymes with "keep," which is about retaining it; and "wake" signals the recovery of consciousness, but it rhymes with "take." Confusing . . . and clear as a bell. And I didn't even know then that "wake" was another word for "funeral."

There was another poem I learned a little later, with a children's-prayer quality to it but cranked up a notch or two. It was called "Heaven-Haven" and was written by the nineteenth-century poet Gerard Manley Hopkins on the occasion of a nun taking her vows.

> I have desired to go
>> Where springs not fail,
> To fields where flies no sharp and sided hail
>> And a few lilies blow.
>
> And I have asked to be
>> Where no storms come,
> Where the green swell is in the havens dumb,
>> And out of the swing of the sea.

When my elder daughter, Sarah, was nine or ten she had to learn a poem in school, and (with maybe just a little help from her father) she chose that one. She learned it perfectly; then she wrote it out very carefully, mounted it on a sheet of paper that she decorated to look like those crocheted cushions that my great aunt used to make, and hung it on the wall. It stayed there throughout her school years (though it was later relegated to the upper gallery by pictures of James Dean in a variety of languid poses). Its tidy rhymes—"go" and "blow," "fail" and "hail," "come" and "dumb," "be" and "sea". . . these are in every sense kid's stuff. Even some of the phrasing seems clumsy or naïve, "child's play." A child could do that . . . though no one would really pretend that a child *could* do that. And yet my child responded to it with a strange delight, as I had: strange, because among other things the poem reveals unexpected connections—between fields and flying, sharp and sided, swing and sea; and delight, because it has a dancer's show-off rhythm to it, with sudden stops and shifts and whirls and wheelings, and a marvellous contradiction to end it all. The very thing heaven haven will protect her from, "the swing of the sea," is what we are left singing.

I know there are clever explanations for my daughter's embrace of this poem, and for the pride of place it held in her room. Cultural and social and probably political explanations: maintaining the great tradition; keeping up in class; pleasing Dad. But there is something else too. Something that has to do with wonder; with a sense of mystery that comes to us with startling clarity; with a self-conscious surrender to forces—of rhythm and rhyme, for example, and the power of the sea and the seasons—that both overwhelm and underwrite us, with reasonings that come as revelations. It has to do with the way in which we are possessed by stories and songs even as they belong to us; the way in which they take hold of our hearts and minds even as they free them up; the way in which we live within them, as well as with them; and the way in which what we know by heart is refreshed each time we repeat it.

We tell two kinds of stories, scary ones and soothing ones. Often they are the same. Like many children, the first stories I heard were nursery rhymes. "One misty, moisty morning," began one of my favourites,

> When cloudy was the weather,
> I chanced to meet an old man,
> Clothed all in leather.

Clothed all in leather,
With cap under his chin,
How do you do, and how do you do,
And how do you do again?

It was a good introduction to literature as well as to life. Not
that I ever met such a man. That was the point: I never would.
And if by some odd chance I were to come across him, I would
probably run like hell. Yet meet him I surely did, every night;
and each evening I looked forward to meeting him one more
time, and to hearing him say exactly the same words all over
again, relishing the rhymes and the rhythms and the ridicu-
lousness of it all. In the strange way of such things, each time
seemed like the first time, caught up in a moment of wonder
that was filled with anticipation and absolute foreknowledge.

Like the ghosts I kept looking for in the bedroom, this
rhyme was a bit scary. But strangely enough, scary stories and
sad songs are often the very ones that make us happy and put
us at ease. This contradiction turns out to be much more fundamental than we might expect. And it is related to another
one, having to do with whether things are real or not.

When I later recited "One Misty, Moisty Morning" to my
children, they joined in the "How do you do's" each night with
something approaching pure glee, greeting the old man as a
stranger even though they had known him—known him by
heart—for as long as they could remember. And they showed
me something else: that their insistence on absolute accuracy in
the recital of stories and songs was not only so the spell wouldn't
be broken; it was also so that they could be absolutely surprised
all over again. We learn more about this much later when we
realize that one mark of a good story or novel is how it rewards
rereading, and how the better we know them the more mysterious they become. Good songs work the same way.

Songs and stories from other cultures have a similar sort of contradictory appeal. It is their foreignness that fascinates us, as the antagonism between Them and Us is transformed into a new relationship between strangeness and familiarity, and between mystery and clarity. The conflict never quite goes away, of course, and a sense of its continuing tension reinforces the hold that such stories have on us.

Throughout our lives, we spend a lot of time among strangers who surprise and sometimes scare us. In a sense, we live there: in the stories and songs of popular culture, which frighten us in all kinds of (some would say quite worrying) ways; and in the secular and sacred myths that shape everything from our racial and national identities to our moral and spiritual responsibilities, myths about strange beginnings or sudden cataclysms—fires and floods, or spiders and coyotes and ravens and other tricksters, or things that go bump in the night. We develop faith in the ability of these strange stories to unsettle us. The strangeness is crucial. It is what first appeals to us in the nonsense of nursery rhymes, and when we learn to bring our acceptance of such nonsense to bear on the strangeness of stories, we are on the way to understanding the world.

Strange tongues make strange, of course, as we have seen with words like *tulku* and *tjakurrpa*. But we needn't go to other languages for this. Unusual words, unusual phrases, and unusual rhythms and rhymes are the stock-in-trade of many of our most cherished songs and stories, from rap and rock to religion. Poetry depends upon strangeness and surprise. Thomas Gray's eighteenth-century poem "Elegy Written in a Country Churchyard" was written in a language nobody ever spoke, so it *must* have always been strange to the millions who admired it, even after they had learned it by heart. Maybe this was the reason it was so popular. Gray himself used to say that "the language of the age is never the language of poetry." Other poets might disagree—certainly Dante (who wrote in his dialect of Italian rather than in conventional Latin) and Chaucer (who wrote in conversational English) would have. But then they wrote about *people* who were strange and wonderful in language that was (for their time) surprisingly straightforward. Even poets whose language seems most colloquial, like Robert Frost, play tricks. "Whose woods these are I think I know," begins one of his most famous poems, using common words of one syllable . . . and very uncommon phrasing. And he ends the poem with the line "And miles to go before I sleep," which he then repeats . . . as if we needed to hear it twice to make sense of it. Maybe we do . . . or maybe hearing it twice makes nonsense of it, making it strange while making it familiar.

In a very public disagreement some years ago in England, over proposals to update the Anglican Book of Common Prayer to make its seventeenth-century language more relevant to the modern reader, many people argued for retaining what one commentator called its "beautiful unordinary language," language that people could not fully understand but in which their faith resided. One of them, the philosopher Mary Warnock, quoted Emmanuel Kant in defence of those "representations of the imagination which induce much thought, yet without the possibility of any definite thought whatever being adequate to them, and which language can never get quite on equal terms with or make completely intelligible." Admitting that to speak in such a way "gives rise to the darkest suspicions," she continued:

> It may be said that I am arguing for an intolerably sentimental view according to which [texts] are to be used simply to suggest certain vague sublimities, to evoke in their hearers certain obscure stirrings of feelings, which cannot be precisely expressed because they are attached to no specific doctrine. Sentimentalism it may be argued is wrong. It

is self-indulgence, and has no connection either with statements that are true or with principles that are morally commendable.

I would argue, on the contrary, that traditional language does indeed arouse sentiment, but it does so only because it makes a direct appeal to our imagination, a power inextricably linked with our emotions. And the appeal to our imaginations is direct precisely because of the unordinariness and antiquity of the language itself. I would further argue that it is only through the power of the imagination that we can apprehend any significance or value in life itself.

This power seems to be most obvious at the point where mystery and clarity converge—in riddles and rhymes, for example—and it is remarkable that it is often when we are most conscious of the arbitrariness and artifice of their form that we surrender to the power of a story or a song.

"We live our life as a tale that is told," says Psalm 90. Oscar Wilde, the great Irish trickster, once rewrote this as "We should live our life as a form of fiction. To be a fact is to be a failure." Our current failure may lie right there; we have become addicted to facts. To feed our habit, we continue to make false choices between the familiar and the strange, the true and the untrue, the worthy and the worthless. We have lost the ability to both surrender to a story and separate ourselves from it, to live in both grief-stricken reality and the grace of the imagination, to both wait for spring and wonder whether it will arrive.

Fortunately, our children haven't lost it. They know how to believe the stories they are told, and how *not* to believe them too; how (as the literary critic Northrop Frye once said) to "send out imaginative roots into that mysterious world between the 'is' and the 'is not' which is where our ultimate freedom lies." And even more surprisingly, they learn it from *us*. We must know *something* about it.

And indeed we do, for we learn very early in our lives about two worlds that are radically separate from each other and yet remarkably similar: the worlds of the imagination and of reality. We learn how to live comfortably in both of them. We learn that neither is the true one, and that sometimes it isn't easy to tell them apart. We learn that we often don't want to, or need to, because the business of living in the real world depends on our living in our imaginations.

Scientists do this, we learn much later, even though they pretend not to. They give wonderful descriptions of atoms as miniature galaxies with colourful planets, curious moons and remarkable orbits . . . and then admit that nobody has ever actually seen one. They say that everything from sentiment to sex is socially constructed—which is to say made up. They talk about the laws of gravity and evolution . . . and then add that these aren't laws at all, just likelihoods. They propose one model of light, as a wave (even though these days, since the idea of the "aether" went out of the window, there is no longer anything for it to wave in); and then, just in case we're not in that kind of mood, they offer another model, as a set of particles (even though they can't explain anything about these particles, not even their size or shape).

Forever, people have listened to the sounds of the streets and the music of the spheres and seen in them patterns and rhythms and melodies and meanings that helped them understand both the earth they live on and their place in the greater scheme of things. To ask whether those patterns and purposes are *really* there is beside the point, for that's how we learn about death and disease and darkness and desire and the power of the wind and the waves and of love and hate and hope and fear, and how we make sense of them. We know that these are real, and we know that they are nothing but stories and songs.

So we teach our children about how stories and songs help us find freedom from false choices. Everyday freedom. The freedom to believe, for example, that the earth is round and also to believe that we are standing right side up, not upside down as we might be if the world really *were* round. The freedom to say "the sun rises in the east and sets in the west" with the confidence we reserve for things that are absolutely true, even though we have known since Copernicus that it is absolutely false.

And we teach them another lesson: that they don't have to have lived in the time of King Arthur or been with Ahab on his quest for Moby Dick or heard Keats's nightingale or seen Wordsworth's daffodils to believe in them, as long as the storytelling imagination brings them to life. All stories are, in some sense, about someplace else or someone else. They take us to imaginary places, with imaginary people. They show us the importance of elsewhere. They may be mirror images of real places and people, but while we are in them we never know.

Two thousand years ago, they used to teach myths and mathematics together. It was a good idea, for children love words and numbers. They learn that the word's the thing, which is to say that it is *not* the thing; and that numbers are real and imagined, both at the same time. I remember the questions my mother used to ask me. Is the word "dog" really a dog? Does the number 4 refer to four dogs, or the fourth dog? Is 0 a number of dogs, or not? And what about -1? How would I draw -1 dog? How many is an infinite number of dogs? Then she'd give me her favourite definition of infinity: "a place where things happen that don't." That's the place of story and song.

In one of the truly awesome achievements of our educational system, we teach those who come to us loving words and numbers to hate poetry and mathematics. What we are in fact teaching them is to make that false choice between reality and the imagination that we talked about earlier, the choice between being marooned on an island and drowning in the sea. Nobody should have to make such a choice. Nobody can. Asking them to do so is a deadly mistake, for among other things it undermines their confidence in themselves, and in the powers—secular or sacred—to which they surrender in a story. That's why the arts are so crucial. They confuse our categories and complicate our choices. They locate us in between, on the border between the true and the not true, the believable and the unbelievable, "both/and" rather than "either/or."

Lunatics, lovers and poets, said Shakespeare, give "to airy nothing a local habitation and a name." He didn't mention scientists, but they certainly belong in this company. Naming things is one of the oldest forms of storytelling, from inscriptions on ancient tombs like King Tutankhamun's to monuments like the Vietnam War Memorial, and from the names of wildflowers in the mountains of the Northwest where I grew up—Tweedy's snowlover, Tiling's monkeyflower, pussypaws or woolly pussytoes—to wonderfully named places like Froze-to-Death Lake and Hell-Roaring Plateau and Sundance Pass and Bumpy Meadows. Sometimes old names hold on long after new ones have been accepted, and create their own contradictions. Sunrise and sunset, for instance, when we know that the sun does no such thing.

Every tradition of stories and songs, in both the sciences and the arts, has allegiances to both reality and the imagination, including that most apparently uncompromising of them all, mathematics. Nobody walks the borderline between what is and what is not with more elegance than mathematicians, whom Bertrand Russell once described as pursuing "a science in which we never know what we are talking about nor whether what we say is true." Children, of course, know a lot about this, especially after they learn to read. Accepting the contradiction that C-A-T is both a cat and not a cat sets them up for all the absurdities of mathematics, from counting on their fingers to calculus.

Counting on our fingers is a good place to start for all sorts of reasons. For a long time, mathematicians resisted numbers that were not like fingers, which is to say were not what they called "real" numbers like 1, 2, or 3 . . . or, for the more advanced, "ratios" of these, such as ½, ⅓, or ¼. Then along came what were called "ir-rational" numbers, numbers (such as the square root of 2) that could not be expressed as real numbers or as fractions of them. They were like imaginary numbers. The eurie-women of mathematics.

Not surprisingly, they caused a lot of problems. Irrational numbers were first discovered by the Pythagoreans a couple of thousand years ago. One of them, a scholar named Hippasus, showed that the side of a square and its diagonal were not what was called "commensurable"; that is, there was no line segment, no matter how small, that would divide evenly into both. It was a Pythagorean way of saying that the length of the diagonal is not a rational number: if the sides of the square are of length 1, for example, then the length of the diagonal must be the square root of 2. This was very upsetting to the Pythagoreans, finger-counters extraordinaire. "Come back to reality," they said. When Hippasus refused, they took him out to sea and threw him overboard.

Even with Hippasus out of the way, irrationals continued to plague the Pythagoreans. Another troublemaker named Hippocrates—the mathematical, not the medical one—brought irrationals into the spotlight again with his attempt to construct a square of equal area to a given circle: that is, to square the circle, to make it rational. A version, one might say, of trying to make dreams come true, or turning Them into Us. For over two thousand years, mathematicians tried to finish what Hippocrates had started. They failed. Finally, in 1882, a

German mathematician named Ferdinand Lindemann proved that it was impossible.

Let's be clear what this means, because it bears directly on how we think about stories and songs and the borderland they occupy between reality and the imagination. It doesn't mean that there doesn't *exist* a square of the same area as a given circle. It's easy to show that there is one. But it will be an *imaginary* existence, not a real one. Imagine a square of light projected on the page beside a given circle. Let's move the projector so that the square has an area smaller than the circle. Then we move the projector back, away from the page, and soon we get a square larger than the circle. We must assume that at some instant the area was the same. But we can't construct such a square, at least not with a compass and a ruler, the limited means that classical geometry puts at our disposal. Just as we can't find Moby Dick out in the Pacific; or Queequeg's home. But they are there.

"Imaginaries in mathematics are a form of the impossible," grumbled the authors of the *Larousse Dictionary* in the 1870s. "Why study such problems, since irrational numbers do not exist?" rejoined Leopold Kronecker, probably the most powerful mathematician in the most powerful mathematics institution of the late nineteenth century, the University of Berlin. "What good is your beautiful investigation?" And his was a fairly generous remark. Most were full of fear and loathing.

Given the late nineteenth-century preoccupation with irrational behaviour, it is interesting that the term "irrational" was used (in German, French and Russian, as well as in English) to refer to numbers that were so strange, and that so completely defied the logic of mathematical realism. Sort of like Sweet William's dream.

But there were even stranger things out there, things that Sweet William would have recognized too. Another class of numbers came to attention around the same time, called "transcendentals." Like irrationals, they had bothered mathematicians for a long time; but unlike them, transcendentals were not even algebraic; that is, they were not the solution of any algebraic equation with rational coefficients, as the square root of 2, for example, is a solution of the equation $x^2 - 2 = 0$. The number "pi," the ratio of a circle's circumference to its diameter, is a transcendental. So is the number "e," the basis of the system of logarithms (or, in mathematical jargon, the limit of $(1 + 1/n)$ to the nth power as "n" increases without limit). These were, if you will pardon the contradiction, the real imaginary numbers. And transcendentals too were proven to "exist," or, more precisely, to exist in the realm of mathematics. But not without some consternation. "I turn aside in horror from this lamentable plague," remarked Charles Hermite, a French mathematician. And he was the one who, in 1873, had devised the proof.

This is all made up, of course. Mathematics, I mean; not my account of it. Well . . . both are, in a way. I said that often it is when we are most conscious of their artifice that we surrender most completely to stories. Sometimes this artifice is ostentatious; but whatever the case, it is always there, and recognizing it helps us understand how stories work. Northrop Frye once suggested that "the appearance of a ghost in *Hamlet* presents the hypothesis 'let there be a ghost in *Hamlet*.' It has nothing to do with whether ghosts exist or not, or whether Shakespeare or his audience thought they did. A reader who quarrels with postulates, who dislikes *Hamlet* because he does not believe that there are ghosts or that people speak in pentameters, clearly has no business in literature." Then he added something else: "The child beginning geometry is presented with a dot and is told, first, that that is a point, and second, that it is not a point. He cannot advance until he accepts both statements at once. It is absurd that that which is no number can also be a number, but the result of accepting the absurdity was the discovery of zero."

Accepting such artifice and absurdity is what children do; not naturally—a mistake we often make—but because we show them how. And although we don't usually use this language, what we show them is how to have faith. John Henry Newman once said that "forms are the food of faith." Soul food. Just as we learn how to eat properly—those table manners once again—so we learn how to believe properly. It is hardly surprising that we do so differently in different societies. But the sense of form, of ceremony, is the same. In this way, zero was discovered by the ancient Babylonians, by the Mayans and by Hindu scholars in India, who are usually credited with popularizing its use sometime after the sixth century.

I didn't read until I was seven or eight. Partly it was because I was too busy checking under the bed for ghosts. But mostly it was because of my first day at school, when I sat frozen with fear at the back of the class. We didn't have kindergarten then, and my mother taught me nonsense rhymes and numbers like zero instead. So this was the real thing, and I had been looking forward to it for a long time. But it wasn't what I expected. Here we were sitting in rows, when all of our short lives we had been plunking ourselves down wherever we wanted. And there was a teacher up there telling us to sit still and keep quiet and pay attention, when up to then our days had been filled with babbling and doodling and travelling all over the place, especially in our imaginations. And we were supposed to answer questions. Up until that moment, we'd been the ones asking them.

It was a ghostly scene. Sounds blurred together as if I were in a dream. Friends became figures in a fog. And then came a fog horn, in the form of the teacher's voice. "What is that?" she asked me, pointing to the letters C-A-T on the wall alongside a picture of a cat. "Nothing," I answered. I knew it was a cat, of course. But I also knew it wasn't a cat. I wasn't budging. I had lost the Battle of Peas-with-a-Knife, and I wasn't going to lose this one.

It took me another couple of years to develop faith in this particular form of nonsense. By the time I did, I had learned how to read and write and to recognize their connection with what I had learned sometime earlier, how to speak and listen. I had learned to be comfortable with a cat that is both there and not there.

I often use the example of tracking to underline how ancient this understanding is, especially if we associate it with reading. The one thing hunters know when they see the track of an animal is that the animal isn't there. That's all they know. And they know that's all they know. This knowledge is at the heart of hunting and tracking. Learning to recognize the difference between a thing and the representation of a thing—the difference between a bear and the word "bear" or the spoor of a bear—is what tracking is all about. It's also what we do when we learn how to read. We learn, as I said a moment ago, that the word's the thing and that it is not the thing.

The folklorist Barre Toelken tells a story about living in southern Utah with his wife's family when he became very ill, contracting pneumonia. There was no doctor, no physician nearby. But there was a medicine man, a native American diagnostician. The family called him in, and he said that Barre was suffering from a particular malady whose cure would be the red-ant ceremony. So a man who was very well versed in that ceremony, a seer, a kind of specialist in the red-ant ceremony, came in and administered it to him. Soon after that he recovered completely.

Not long after this, Toelken was talking to his father-in-law, and he was very curious about what had taken place. He said, "I wonder about the red-ant ceremony. Why is it that the diagnostician prescribed that particular ceremony for me?" His father-in-law looked at him and said, "Well, it was obvious to him that there were red ants in your system, and so we had to call in a seer to take the red ants out of your system." At this point, he became incredulous and said, "Yes, but surely you don't mean that there were red ants inside of me." His father-in-law looked at him for a moment, and then said, "Not ants, but ants."

The Kiowa writer N. Scott Momaday, author of the novel *House Made of Dawn*, once used this story to describe how a traditional Indian view of nature involves bringing people and nature into alignment, first of all to achieve some kind of moral order and then to enable a person "not only to see what is really there, but also to see what is *really* there." Unless we understand this distinction, he added, we will have difficulty understanding the Indian view of the natural world.

Before we write all this off as native romanticism or New Age nonsense, we should remember that this kind of contradiction can be found in all cultural traditions—it is the basis of story and song in the sciences as well as in the arts—and unless we understand what Toelken and Momaday are saying, we may have difficulty understanding not just the Indian, but *any* view of the natural world, including our own. And we will find it impossible to understand how stories and songs and ceremonies of belief actually work.

During the late summer and early fall when I was going to university, I worked as a big-game hunting guide. One year, I was on a trip in the southeast of British Columbia with an Indian by the name of Camille Joseph. He was chief of the Kootenai band, a man with a wonderful sense of humour and a legendary reputation—his nickname, misspelled on the walls of bush cabins throughout the mountain and river region that we called the Kootenays, was Kemeal the Prophet. He was supposed to be able to predict the weather and the ways of the woods. On our first morning out, he came running back from the creek near where we were camped with exciting news for the hunters, a wide-eyed group from Louisiana. "I've just seen a grizzly," he said breathlessly. Then, after a long silence filled with the unspoken authority of his Indian heritage, he added, "I recognized it from some pictures I saw in *National Geographic* magazine."

A few days later, as we were walking out to check on the horses, Camille told me where he *had* first met a grizzly—not in *National Geographic*, of course, but not up Bear Creek, either. His first encounter, he said—with the seriousness of someone for whom hunting was a way of life—had been in a story told him by his father, and repeated many times. He first learned how to hunt not from going out in the woods but from listening to his father, over and over again. His imagination was educated in the realities of hunting before he ever walked up the trail.

Let me follow this trail a bit further. The Canadian folk singer Ian Tyson has a song about the cowboy painter Charles Russell in which he tells of the ways in which Russell set down the beauty of the western plains and the burdens of everyday life in those twilight days of the prairie frontier. "God hung the stars over Judith basin," the song begins . . . and Russell painted them. He also painted the great herds of buffalo, the riding of broncs and the roping of cattle, the cow camps and round-ups and stampedes. He painted the people of the plains, not only the ranchers and the rodeo cowboys but the Piegan and the Sioux and the Crow, who had been living in the region for millennia. And he painted the extraordinary sunsets. Especially those sunsets. And so,

When the Lord called Charlie
To His home up yonder,
He says, "Kid Russell,
I got a job for you.
You're in charge of sunsets

Up in old Montana,
'Cause I can't paint them
Quite as good as you."

A cowboy fancy, to be sure. But it also embodies a powerful
and perennial conviction that works of art bring things to life,
that a portrait can somehow be more real than a person, that
truth is much closer to beauty, and perhaps to goodness too,
than our rational minds might like to admit, and that stories
and songs and paintings and photographs and drumming and
dancing and all our various forms of imaginative expression
shape the world and nourish the spirit.

For thousands of years, singers and storytellers have wondered about the relationships between real and imagined
worlds, between life and art. The history of art and literature
is a history of a feud—or perhaps I should say a dialogue—
between what are sometimes called mirroring and making,
which is to say between the notions that art imitates reality and
that it creates it. And many of our conflicts across cultures
come down to a disagreement over whether stories and songs
create or merely communicate thought and feeling.

Just to show that cowboys have something in common
with so-called high culture, let me end this chapter by turning
to one of the great jugglers of contradictions, Oscar Wilde. In
an essay called "The Decay of Lying," he bemoaned the fact
that there were so few good liars around, liars who told lies
purely for pleasure rather than for profit (as lawyers and jour-
nalists do, he added mischievously); liars who told the stories
and sang the songs that we call novels and plays and poems as
well as the older ones who painted on rocks and carved stone
and wood in elaborate designs. Wilde talked about how we see
reality in ways that are determined by our imagination, and
especially by the imaginative representations of art. And then,
in his characteristically outrageous fashion, he offered proof.

Where, if not from the Impressionists, do we get those wonderful brown fogs that come creeping down our streets, blurring the gas-lamps and changing the houses into monstrous shadows? . . . The extraordinary change that has taken place in the climate of London during the last ten years is entirely due to a particular school of Art. . . . Things are because we see them, and what we see, and how we see it, depends on the arts that have influenced us. To look at a thing is very different from seeing a thing. One does not see anything until one sees its beauty. Then, and only then, does it come into existence. At present, people see fogs, not because there are fogs, but because poets and painters have taught them the mysterious loveliness of such effects. There may have been fogs for centuries in London. I dare say there were. But no one saw them, and so we do not know anything about them. They did not exist until art had invented them. Now, it must be admitted fogs are carried to excess. They have become the mere mannerism of a clique, and the exaggerated realism of their method gives dull people bronchitis. Where the cultured catch an effect, the uncultured catch cold.

With all the wit there's also wisdom in this argument and in its most famous aphorism, Wilde's signature song: "Life imitates art." How do we tell the difference, especially when the imitation is good? That, too, is an old question. The Chinese sage Chuang Tzu, put it into a fable about himself (using his given name Chou instead of his title Tzu).

Once Chuang Chou dreamt he was a butterfly, a butterfly flitting and fluttering around, happy with himself and doing as he pleased. He didn't know he was Chuang Chou. Suddenly he woke up and there he was, solid and unmistakable Chuang Chou. But he didn't know if he was Chuang Chou who had dreamt he was a butterfly, or a butterfly dreaming he was Chuang Chou.

The closer we come to this borderline between art and life, or "is" and "is not," or truth and lies, the better able we are to recognize the arbitrariness of both. And the better able we will be to reimagine Them and Us.

SEVEN

Truth and Consequences

IN ALL STORYTELLING, the more fascinating the fictions—scientists call them theories—the more sense the facts make. As though to underline this, our English word "fact" comes from the same root as "fiction;" both mean "something made up."

The English writer Charles Tomlinson once said that artists "lie for the improvement of truth." Oscar Wilde proposed that "the telling of beautiful untrue things" is the proper aim of storytelling, and that the liar "is the very basis of civilized society." Plato wanted to keep poets and playwrights out of his ideal republic because they indulged in mimicry and were therefore immoral. In some traditions, singers and storytellers have embraced such accusations, welcoming them as a signal of their freedom from the distractions of conventional morality. In others, they have insisted that they are the only ones who tell the truth and show us how to live our lives.

Stories and songs always tell of places where things happen that don't and of happenings that are not happening. They are true, like the "true north strong and free" of the Canadian national anthem. And they are not true; just ask aboriginal people about whether that song truly describes *their* "home and native land." The turtle's back, which to the Anishinaabe of the northern woodlands is where we live, is just a fable to many of us, while to them it is as true as the sunrise and all of modern science.

We all grow up with stories and songs about strange things, things we have never seen. They are real the way the people we meet in books are real, the way that old man clothed all in leather is real, or red ants, or atoms, or imaginary numbers. Maybe "more real," Derek Walcott once insisted, "than the heat and the oleander [of his home in St. Lucia], because they live in memory. There is a memory of imagination in literature which has nothing to do with actual experience, which is, in fact, another life, and that experience of the imagination will continue to make actual the quest of a medieval knight or the bulk of a white whale."

These days we often assume that the images to which we give wide public assent must be familiar ones, or at least forged by a local blacksmith. But none of us has ever seen a medieval knight like King Arthur, nor a white whale like Moby Dick. And one of our most compelling contemporary images is of something that almost nobody has seen, at least not in its natural habitat. A lion. The Lion King. The British Lion. The Lion of Rastafari. The Lion of Judah. A lion from a book. The Bible, maybe; or, like Camille Joseph's bear, from *National Geographic*. Certainly *not* from the Caribbean, where the lion is an icon of Rastafari; or from the British Isles, where it is an icon of imperial power; or from Broadway, where it has made a new kind of mark for itself. And yet, as E. L. Doctorow would say, it is now. Many of us might say something the same about bears and horses. We may have met some in real life, but the ones we know best and like most are the ones we meet in stories like "The Three Bears" or *Black Beauty*.

At the beginning of the book he called *Another Life*, the life of the imagination, Derek Walcott tells the story of the great Renaissance artist Giotto, whose paintings were said to convey a keener sense of the real world than reality itself. Giotto began his life as a shepherd, sketching sheep as he watched them in the field, so he was often celebrated as an artist with roots in the natural world. But he always insisted that it was art that made him love nature, and that he painted not because of his pastoral life but because of the paintings he saw of it. The paintings showed him how to be surprised by familiar things, how to make them strange.

From cave paintings by Neolithic hunters and tall tales told by early fishing folk, this is what art has always been about. When the avant-garde French artist Marcel Duchamp submitted a urinal, titled *Fountain*, to the Society of Independent Artists for a show in New York in 1917, he put a conspicuously "useful" item alongside ostentatiously "useless" works of art and forced people to look at it in a new way and see its unordinariness. The artists and hunters who painted horses on the walls of the Chauvet Cave in France thirty thousand years ago were not painting horses and buffalo; they were painting *paintings* of horses and buffalo. They knew all about the difference between reality and the imagination.

This difference sometimes produces conflict, mostly because the line between the strange and the familiar is so culturally determined. The nineteenth-century Danish novelist Jens Peter Jacobsen, who wrote a story called "Two Worlds" about living between two "realities," said that he wished his language would have allowed him to call it "Two World."

One of my favourite stories in this vein is one my grandfather used to tell, about a meeting between Colonel Macleod, the head of the newly established North West Mounted Police, and Crowfoot, Chief of the Blackfoot, in southern Alberta in the 1870s. Colonel Macleod spoke first, paying tribute to Crowfoot and his people, asking their permission to come into Indian country, praising the chief's statesmanship in leading his people in those difficult times, and promising to safeguard them from the menace of the new barbarians, the whiskey traders and Indian haters of the Wild West. Macleod was courteous and concise. He spoke for about three minutes. "We are glad to be here," he said. The legendary half-breed Jerry Potts translated, and Crowfoot listened carefully.

Then Chief Crowfoot began a long speech in Blackfoot, during which he picked up a handful of earth, motioned in the direction of the heavens, embraced several of his companions, pointed enviously at the North West Mounted Police horses, and described a herd going over the ancient buffalo jump—called Head-Smashed-In—just across the way from where they stood. He went on, and on, and on, for over half an hour. Eventually, worried by Crowfoot's increasingly energetic—and maybe belligerent?—gestures, Macleod turned to Potts and asked, "What's he saying, Jerry?" "Damn glad too," Potts replied.

Two ways of welcoming, from conventions in which courtesies counted but were bound into different languages and different ceremonial traditions. Does this mean that Colonel Macleod and Chief Crowfoot lived in two worlds? I grew up with this question, and I still think the answer is yes and no.

Let me put this question differently. Was one tradition truer than the other? At the beginning of *The Odyssey*, Odysseus the storyteller is described as a man of twists and turns; sometimes he is bluntly called a liar. Achilles, the straight arrow, says in *The Iliad* that he "hates that man like the very Gates of Death who says one thing and holds another in his heart." It is a textbook definition of someone saying something ironic, and folks who do that are often pretty irritating; but in this case Achilles is talking about Odysseus, who isn't given to irony at all. Odysseus has come to persuade Achilles to join Agamemnon in the attack on Troy, and he tells him less than the whole truth about what Agamemnon thinks of him. A white lie. We tell them all the time in order not to hurt people's feelings. You could say Odysseus was just being nice; after all, he was a charmer, a spellbinder. So what's the difference between telling a lie and telling the truth? Or between accepting something as true and calling someone a liar? Good manners?

Perhaps. But then what is the test of good manners? Who decides whether we will eat peas with a knife or a fork?

Who decides whether to believe Mary Johnson or her song? Who determines the courtesies of first contact, or of anything else for that matter? The tradition itself, as my father implied when he said I should learn Ukrainian, and as the Iroquois elder was reminded when he tried to tell the Great Law of the Haudenosaunee in English instead of Cayuga? Or does the individual singer or storyteller determine decorum? Sometimes they themselves are unsure not only of their motives but also of whether they have discovered or invented—a.k.a. stolen or fabricated—their stories. In the 1930s, members of a Federal Writers' Project interviewed a number of people in New Mexico who knew Billy the Kid. Some claimed personal knowledge of events which it turned out had never happened. They had been invented by fiction writers and "borrowed" by those who told the stories; but after a while they believed them to be true, and believed them to be theirs.

Unfortunately for storytellers, we live in a world in which the truth has consequences, and so do lies. In a book called *The Stories That Shape Us*, the American writer Teresa Jordan tells of growing up with a story about her father's family, told to her first by her grandfather Sunny Jordan. He was "a ranchman of the old school," she says, "gruff and not given to small talk. Too many bad horses and too much bad weather had crippled him some; later, he had a series of strokes. . . . He frightened me, as he did all children." And yet he caught their imaginations, like the old man clothed all in leather did. This was the story he told.

His father had been born in Maryland around the middle of the last century. He had wanted to join his brothers fighting the Civil War, but he was only fourteen and his father refused permission. So he ran away; but before he got to the front, the war was over. Unable to return home, he headed west, working his way across the country, turning his hand to a wide range of jobs, and finally ending up on a ranch in Wyoming. Eventually the owner died, owing him several years' wages, and in the rough trade of the West, Jordan received title to his land in payment. He added to it over the next few years, and eventually it became the Jordan family ranch. But he remained estranged from his parents, never even writing home to let them know he was alive until he had built up a sizable spread and made a success of himself.

It was the family story, but it was also the history of the West. Like all histories, this one shaped the Jordan family as each new generation of men rebelled against their fathers and tried to mirror the stubborn independence and fierce pride of that great-grandfather, a fourteen-year-old runaway driven by destiny and doggedness to the frontier, there to do it alone.

Except that it hadn't happened that way at all. Some years after Sunny died, Teresa Jordan discovered a packet of letters written by her great-grandfather to his father back in Maryland. These letters told a very different story. He had been four years old when the Civil War had ended; he left home to go out west with his family's blessing at the age of twenty-five; he wrote fond letters home, telling his father all about his travels and how homesick he was. He did work at an assortment of jobs in Wyoming, but he hated it. And when his boss offered him a chance to buy some cattle, his father loaned him the money. Later, after he had done well, he sent money back home to help his family. A young man who had gone west when he was ready, been homesick, needed help, got it, and then gave back. As Teresa Jordan tells it:

> I cannot describe the revelation that these two stories, laid side by side, provided for me. It was the first time I fully understood how much our stories shape us, how much we are the stories we tell about ourselves. My grandfather had died without making the arrangements that would have allowed the ranch to pass to my father. Like many western

families—like many American families—mine had a history of fathers fighting sons. And as I thought about the generations of tension that had distanced [them], I thought: how could it have been any different? They had all measured themselves and each other against someone who had never existed.

I'm certain Sunny never changed his father's story. Rather, he absorbed it from the culture at large. Owen Wister's Virginian, the hero of the most popular Western ever written, was a fourteen-year-old orphan, as were many of the heroes of the Horatio Alger stories. These orphans turned up in so many popular novels and have been absorbed into so many family stories that one would think the trails west were blazed by armies of homeless fourteen-year-olds. My family told one story about ourselves. It severed the bonds between us and put us off the land.

The link between father and son was severed by a story, and the land that had been in the Jordan family for four generations was lost. Teresa Jordan's tale is both a testament to the power of tales, and an elegy for the loss of land and the livelihood that goes with it. Like all stories, her grandfather's story had the power to make things happen. Because of it, he lost his father and his son, and the family lost their land.

The portmanteau word "semiotics" was popularized a few years ago by Umberto Eco, the author of the novel *The Name of the Rose*. The word comes originally from medical diagnostics, and simply means the interpretation of "signs." Hippocrates, the founder of medical science, first used it to refer to a patient's symptoms; and semiotics has become not so much the study of truthtelling as of everything that can be used in order to deceive us. If something cannot be used to tell a lie, Eco once suggested, it cannot be used to tell the truth; it cannot in fact be used to "tell" at all.

The Canadian storyteller Dan Yashinsky recalls his Romanian grandmother saying, "When in doubt, fake it. Go through the motions. Act like you know what you are doing." Though it may not be popular to say so, that's what all singers and storytellers do; and that's why songs like "Amazing Grace" and "Bridge Over Troubled Waters" and national anthems like "The Star-Spangled Banner" or the "Marseillaise" have such a hold on us. When we are in doubt—and I think to some extent we almost always are when we sing these songs—they show us how to fake it.

Perhaps we should take comfort from the fact that the central figures in so many storytelling traditions are tricksters, from the classical god Hermes and the West African (and now West Indian) spider Anansi to the crafty Coyote and unreliable Raven of native America. At the end of *A Portrait of the Artist as a Young Man*, James Joyce has Stephen Dedalus vow "to forge the uncreated conscience of his race." The word "forge" is carefully chosen to catch the contradiction: it's both a forging and a forgery.

The everyday world of gravity and genetic codes and evolution and the energy of atoms is riddled with such fakery—which, in order to keep the peace, we might prefer to call contradictions. Scientists, who are among our greatest singers and storytellers, revel in them. As we have seen, they give wonderful descriptions of atoms and then they admit that they have never seen one; their current models, in fact, are more like those clouds of possibility in the sky in which we see images of horses or swans or Aunt Eileen. Scientists are always uncertain about absolute truths, just as they are about the essential nature of reality. One of the fundamentals of science is that hypotheses can never be proven absolutely true. They must be workable, of course, and scientists sometimes *say* they are true, as much for our sake as theirs. But good scientists have a remarkably high level of comfort with the ultimate unprovability of their theories . . . even though many of them have a remarkably low tolerance for those who question them in practice. And so, just as we learn how to believe singers and storytellers, we learn how to believe scientists. With our imaginations.

The original Greek word for a trick was *dolos,* and the first trick was baiting a hook for a fish. Hermes began his career when he was one day old by stealing cattle from Apollo which he then barbecued but didn't eat, thereby making the point that some things are valuable not because they are useful but because they are special—or, if you are a thief, because they belong to someone else. Lewis Hyde, in a book called *Trickster Makes This World,* catches the character of the imaginative sleight of hand I am talking about when he says: "Hermes is neither the god of the door leading out nor the god of the door leading in—he is the god of the hinge."

Earlier, I used the word "faith" to talk about our response to the songs we sing and the stories we tell. Scientists know about faking it; that's why they are our favourite truth tellers. But they also know about faith, and that's why they get along across cultures much better than the rest of us. As the scientist John Polanyi once remarked, "It is not the laws of physics that make science possible but the unprovable proposition that there exists a grand design underlying the physical world. And not just any old 'grand design' but one that is accessible to the limited sense and modest reasoning powers of the species to which we belong. Scientists subscribe with such conviction to this article of faith that they are willing to commit a lifetime to the pursuit of scientific discovery." This is not a lot different from the surrender to articles of faith that takes place every day in religions all over the world. It is our common embrace of those moments of wonder that I mentioned at the beginning of this book.

Let's go back for a moment to Mary Johnson's song and Judge McEachern's court. For the Gitksan, the *ada'ox* that

Mary Johnson performed was proof of the truth of the events it described: that is to say, the storytelling tradition itself, with its stylized language and its ceremonial protocol, was its own guarantor of truth. Whatever was done within that tradition, provided it was done *properly*, was true. The truth had to do with ceremony, not evidence.

An extreme instance of this kind of dedication to the proprieties of story and song occurred several years ago among the Gitksan, when an elder was asked to speak and sing his *ada'ox*, known only to him. Because of various circumstances in the community—some people had moved away for a time, others had become uninterested—nobody had heard it for years. The elder was old, and ill, and not likely to live much longer. He needed to tell the tales so that they would not be forgotten, and so that a central part of the history of his people would not be lost.

He refused. He said that the people who tradition prescribed should listen to the story—certain nephews and aunts and cousins—were all dead; and although he could put on the appropriate regalia and go to the designated spot at just the right time, it wouldn't work. It would be just words. All kinds of arguments were put to him to get him to change his mind. But he wouldn't be persuaded. His refusal had nothing to do with denying authority or offending the ancestors. It had to do with making meaning and telling the truth. To perform his *ada'ox* without the right people there to listen would be meaningless and untrue, he insisted.

So, unlike the hereditary chief of the Cayuga, he died without speaking. And with him went a whole cycle of stories and songs that had been handed down and held secure for thousands of years, a great library holding knowledge that existed nowhere else in the world.

This commitment to convention is part of a very old tradition of truthtelling. The story properly told, or the song properly sung, *is* true. Propriety counts for everything on such occasions, as it does in ceremonies such as witnessing to faith in congregation or to facts in a court of law. Proper form is the key: the proprieties in each are different—one typically passionate and possessed, the other straightforward and rational—but the conventions themselves are crucial for the truthtelling. We notice this especially when the traditions are different from ours.

What, then, is the test of truth? Reality, or the imagination? Surely we wouldn't want to say that the story of Romeo and Juliet is not true just because it didn't happen. It did. I *saw* it happen. That's a fact. And I cried. That's a fact too. It may also be a fact that people were never born in the world who talk or act like Romeo and Juliet. But that's a relatively uninteresting fact, and it certainly doesn't diminish the truth of *Romeo and Juliet* to me when I watch it well performed on stage or film, any more than the idea of a round earth (or should I say the reality of it?) diminishes the reality (or should I say the idea?) of a sunset, especially a Montana sunset painted by Charles Russell. Was there ever a ship called the *Pequod* with a captain called Ahab? Sure there was; and his first mate, Starbuck, the practical one who said that they would make more money by going after a lot of small whales rather than one big one, later founded a chain of coffee houses.

I think of an anecdote about Laurence Olivier, from the making of the film *Marathon Man*. Dustin Hoffman was exhausted, having shot a scene for which he had prepared himself by running until he could hardly walk, and staying up so late he could hardly speak. Olivier had just portrayed his character, a maliciously evil Nazi dentist, with breathtaking authenticity and apparently no preparation at all. "My dear boy," said Olivier to Hoffman, "why don't you try acting?"

Fake it. We should never underestimate the power of the imagination; or as James Joyce said, the appeal of a good forgery.

In *Ulysses*, Joyce gives a comical catalogue of Irish heroes to demonstrate what this is sometimes all about. He begins with a portrait that conjures up the exaggerations of Homer's own storytelling.

> The figure . . . was that of a broadshouldered deepchested stronglimbed frankeyed redhaired freely freckled shaggy-bearded widemouthed largenosed longheaded deepvoiced barekneed brawnyhanded hairylegged ruddyfaced sinewy-armed hero. From shoulder to shoulder he measured several ells and his rocklike mountainous knees were covered, as was likewise the rest of his body wherever visible, with a strong growth of tawny prickly hair in hue and toughness similar to the mountain gorse. The widewinged nostrils, from which bristles of the same tawny hue projected, were of such capaciousness that within their cavernous obscurity the fieldlark might easily have lodged her nest. The eyes in which a tear and a smile strove ever for mastery were of the dimensions of a goodsized cauliflower. . . .
>
> He wore a long unsleeved garment of recently flayed oxhide reaching to the knees in a loose kilt and this was bound about his middle by a girdle of plaited straw and rushes. . . . From [t]his girdle hung a row of seastones which dangled at every movement of his portentous frame and on these were graven with rude yet striking art the tribal images of many Irish heroes and heroines of antiquity, Cuchulain, Conn of hundred battles, Niall of nine hostages, Brian of Kincora . . . Shane O'Neill, Father John Murphy . . . the Village Blacksmith, Captain Moonlight, Captain Boycott, Dante Alighieri, Christopher Columbus, . . . the Mother of the Maccabees, the Last of the Mohicans, the Rose of Castille, the Man for Galway, the Man that Broke the Bank at Monte Carlo, the Man in the Gap, the Woman Who Didn't, Benjamin Franklin, Napoleon

Bonaparte, John L. Sullivan, Cleopatra, Savoureen Deelish, Julius Caesar, Paracelsus, Sir Thomas Lipton, William Tell, Michelangelo, . . . Muhammad, The Bride of Lammermoor, Peter the Hermit, Peter the Packer, Dark Rosaleen, Patrick W. Shakespeare, Brian Confucius, Murtagh Gutenberg . . .

Black or white, man or woman, Protestant or Catholic, Muslim or Christian, Canadian or Macedonian, we all have heard lists that are a lot like this.

The novelist Halldór Laxness, on the 1100th anniversary of the settlement of his native Iceland, picked up on this kind of fanciful catalogue when he suggested that Icelanders have descended as much from books as they have from men. He was referring to the great sagas that have a central place in their literary tradition, and which have become their history, true within one of those narratives of nationhood that we all live by. Laxness poked fun at the invention of Icelandic genealogies which traced pedigrees back to Homer's Troy, and he described the storytelling of one Arngrimur Jonsson, who in the late sixteenth century set out to counteract the belief that Icelanders are the descendants of robbers, murderers and slave owners with another version, straight from the sagas of medieval Iceland, in which they come from a long line of aristocratic heroes, noble commoners and poets. In due course, Arngrimur's history changed northerners' sense of themselves. It inspired nationalist uprisings that led to independence for many Scandinavian nations. It also encouraged assumptions of Nordic superiority, including the misrepresentations of Nazi tyranny. So be it, said Laxness, sadly. That's the way with stories and songs.

"Before Arngrimur's time," continued Laxness,

nobody seems to have asked whether the sagas were "true" or not. It is not very likely that the problem had ever come

up. Arngrimur was the one who discovered that question, as
well as the answer to it: all true. To a people enjoying true
literature, it was an irrelevant question to ask, and the
answer incomprehensible; a question inconsistent with your
mental makeup—and with the world you live in. Like all
great art, the saga is too great a truth in itself to be com-
pared with reality. Such people were never born in the
world who talk, or for that matter act, like the characters of,
say, *Njal's Saga*.

Or like Romeo and Juliet. But just try to tell me that they
aren't true.

How then to judge the truth? How to decide whether we
are in the realm of the imagination or in reality? One trick is to
see things from different perspectives, recognizing that stories
and songs both express their truths in more or less direct communication and reveal them in words and images that we must
interpret. Our unease with other people's stories is often
caught up in our uncertainty about whether they are expressing
or revealing their truths; and this uncertainty is kept alive in
the language we use to talk about truthtelling. The word
"witness," for instance, refers both to the testimony given and
to the individual giving it; in the Bible, the Greek word for
which "witness" is the usual translation is the root of our
English word "martyr." This sets truthtelling alongside suffering, which seems to settle responsibility onto the teller rather
than the tale, with the test of truth being the teller's credibility.
But we know there is more to it than that.

The Bible is interesting in its handling of questions about
truthtelling. In Chinook, the West Coast language of contact
between natives and newcomers, the word *kloosh* meant
"good"; so a translation of the Bible published by the London
British and Foreign Bible Society in 1912 referred to the gospels
as "Kloosh Yiems." Good Stories. In the New Testament

Gospel of St. John, where the problems of witnessing are more prominent than anywhere else, one of the central discussions concerns the truth of what Jesus says about himself. On the one hand, there is his comment: "If I bear witness of myself, my witness is not true." On the other hand, when the Pharisees put that comment back to him, his response was: "Though I bear record of myself, yet my record is true: for I know whence I came, and whither I go."

These two statements make both Odysseus and James Joyce look straightforward. But behind their blunt contradiction is an illuminating uncertainty: when we give testimony, it is always to some degree testimony about ourselves in the sense that our credibility is being judged. But it is also testimony about whoever or whatever certifies or backs our statements (the way gold or the Gross National Product backs paper currency). In Jesus' case, it is God (rather than the Pharisees, though they assume it is them). Most often, it is the ceremony itself, which is to say the form and function of the story or song.

Earlier, I mentioned the word |garube, meaning "the happening that is not happening," used by Khoekhoe hunters and herders in southern Africa to mark the beginning of a story. The root of |garube is |garu, which means "inconsistent speech by a sober person," the kind of speech or story that hovers between the arbitrary and the deliberate. It is not necessarily serious; and it is assumed that a story in such speech will be understood only by those who recognize the uncertainty of motive behind it, like the uncertainty between trickery and thievery.

There is a prefix, |gu, which is sometimes used to intensify this sense of contradiction, and which refers to a story told by a dying person to someone else as their inheritance. Stories don't get much more serious, or more motivated, than that. The prefix and the root together bring us to an interesting convergence. The combination |gu |garu is used by Khoekhoe speakers to refer to stories that nestle between fact and fiction, between intentional seriousness and unconscious fantasy; and some Khoekhoe speakers in Namibia, who have been Christians for hundreds of years, use it to refer to the Bible.

One of the ways in which storytellers finesse the line between the true and the untrue is with humour and exaggeration. Each is bound up in cultural conventions, but both are common in all cultures. They often bring reality and the imagination into closer contact, and in doing so illustrate how stories give us a way of seeing the truth even when they are not exactly telling us the truth. The so-called magical realism of Latin American storytellers brings us closer than we recognize to the everyday.

With my old friends the cowboys, the same was true. They accepted the crippling and sometimes deadly uncertainties of their lives with a fatalism that was tragic and comic by turns, generating a tradition of tall tales and humour that is one of our great legacies of story and song. Anyone who has heard a good rodeo announcer will recognize its latest version. There was much by way of wonder and a good deal of wit in their stories and songs, with the cowboy being alternately amused and amazed by the ways of his world. And in their expression of very human hopes and fears, there was an illustration of how lives so different from ours could seem to have something in common.

The weather held special terrors and inspired a special kind of imagining for cowboys on the *llanos* and the *pampas* and the plains and the prairies. In the North American southwest and northwest, many cattle outfits did not carry tents, and the men took the storms on their Stetsons. One cowboy recalled a night in a plains hailstorm when he had to strip the saddle off his horse and hide beneath it for several hours to protect himself. Of course, if you believe this—and it's undoubtedly true—then you might believe anything. So the tales got taller.

There was the time a gale took away the camp cookstove . . . and returned the next day for the lids and the poker. That was on the same day that the wind was so strong from the west that the sun was three hours late going down. There were other things as strange and as scary, but true. In a summer storm, heat lightning would play across the horns of the herd in an eerie blue glow, beads of static electricity forming on the manes of the horse and rolling down the moustaches of the riders, and balls of fire occasionally knocking a man off his horse. Suddenly the song "Ghosts Riders in the Sky" takes on new meaning. In the fall, blue northers (so called because of the blue of the threatening sky) would blow up out of nowhere and send the cattle stampeding, while the half-frozen cowboys pursued them through the black stormy night. And then there were the winters on the northern plains. One time it got so cold that the thermometer dropped to 95 degrees below zero. The foreman came out to give the cowboys their orders, but the words froze as they came out of his mouth, and they had to break them off one by one so they could tell what he was saying.

There are more reliable accounts, making even *The Odyssey* look like a Mediterranean cruise. My grandfather told about how a friend of his froze his toes in bed one night in Alberta, in a winter when everyone lost at least half their herd of cattle. In *Wolf Willow,* the prairie writer Wallace Stegner describes an all too typical Saskatchewan scene.

> Icy nights, days when a bitter wind lashed and stung the face with a dry sand of snow, mornings when the crust flashed up a glare so blinding that they rode with eyes closed to slits and looked at the world through their eyelashes. There was one afternoon when the whole world was overwhelmed under a white freezing fog, when horses, cattle, clothes, wagon, grew a fur of hoar frost and the herd they had

gathered had to be held together in spooky white darkness mainly by ear.

On bright days they were all nearly blind, in spite of painting their cheekbones with charcoal and riding with hats pulled clear down; if they could see to work at all, they worked with tears leaking through swollen and smarting lids. Their faces grew black with sun and glare, their skin and lips cracked as crisp as the skin of a fried fish, and yet they froze.

My favourite cold-weather cowboy story is by Charles Russell, who used to tell about a friend of his who left a poker game in Great Falls, Montana, and froze to death on the street. When listeners would express sympathy, Charlie would say, "Oh, that wasn't so bad. We hung a lantern on his ear and used him for a lamppost all winter."

And then there are the stories about horses. In some ways, it's no wonder they end up at the centre of the conflict between the useful and the useless. For thousands of years, horses have represented the extravagance of the imagination pushing back against the pressure of reality. These are horses that win battles and horses that represent wealth and power, horses that exemplify traditions of skill and strength and grace and beauty, horses that are prized for their colour and conformation as much as for their courage and craft, horses that fly in the air and horses that work the land. Often the very same horses.

The iconography of horses has sometimes focused on their utility—for war, for travel, for hunting and farming and ranching. To be sure, the idea of horses as useful runs deep. But it is certainly not the only idea. For millennia, horses have graced the walls of caves and castles, their form and colour and movement providing inspiration rather than income. They have represented ideals of beauty and elegance as well as of discipline and strength and courage. And while the recreation and sports in which they feature—from racing and driving and jumping and dressage to buzkashi and polo and the skill of the rodeo circuit and the acrobatics of circuses—all celebrate useful skills, they also embody something of what the American poet Wallace Stevens used to call "essential gaudiness."

At the end of *Walden,* Thoreau reflects on the need to go beyond the limits of moderation. In one of his wonderfully contradictory remarks he worries that he has not been extravagant enough in his praise of simplicity, and he appeals for a commitment to excess, to wandering from the path of caution and common sense.

> It is a ridiculous demand which England and America make, that you shall speak so that they can understand you. Neither men nor toadstools grow so. . . . As if Nature could support but one order of understandings. . . . I fear chiefly lest my expression may not be extravagant enough, may not wander far enough beyond the narrow limits of my daily experience, so as to be adequate to the truth of which I have been convinced. Extravagance. It depends on how you are yarded. The migrating buffalo, who seeks new pastures in another latitude, is not extravagant like the cow which kicks over the pail, leaps the cowyard fence, and runs after her calf, in milking time. . . . Why level downward to our dullest perception always, and praise that as common sense. The commonest sense is the sense of men asleep, which they express by snoring.

This extravagance is the imaginative excess, the more-than-enough that is at the heart of stories and songs. It is the quality that counteracts what Thoreau called a life of quiet desperation; that takes us beyond the true and the untrue, the useful and the useless; and that keeps us safe and sane by celebrating the unsafe and the things that defy common sense.

PART IV ⤙   *Riddles*

and Charms

EIGHT

Riddles

"THERE WILL BE PEOPLE HERE who think the world is round. And people who think the world is flat. Same people." This was Mortimo Planno, also known as Ras Kumi, at the beginning of a gathering of Rastafarian elders in Kingston, Jamaica. "As it is written in the Psalms of David, 'To Every Song is a Sign,' and I an I always Sing the Songs of the Signs of the Time," he added, insisting (in a long tradition of visionary thinking) that the past portrayed in the Old Testament *is* present, and that Africans in the Americas *are* the Israelites in Babylon. This is pure metaphor, the basis of all belief, and it almost begs us to make a choice: believe it or not. The challenge is to believe it *and* not. Not ants, but ants.

Riddles—often by way of nursery rhymes and trickster tales—give us our first lessons in how to meet this challenge. The word "riddling" comes from the same root as "reading," and reading, as we have seen, depends on our ability to recognize that a word is not what it is and yet it is. Riddling, for its part, requires us to make sense of what seems like nonsense. What grows smaller the more you add to it? A hole. What's a cherry without a stone, and a chicken without a bone? A cherry blossom and an egg, says the old folk song. What is rooted in the ground and dances in the air? A daffodil, answers Wordsworth, in one of the best-known poems in the English language.

A riddle was once put by a bunch of young boys to Homer: "What we've caught and killed we've left behind. What has escaped us we've brought with us. What have we been hunting?" Homer couldn't solve the riddle, so the story goes, and he was deeply upset, not so much because of his inability—he was by reputation the wisest man in ancient Greece and much too smart to be bothered by his own ignorance—but because of the dilemma he now faced. He knew that what the boys told him was true, for that was the convention of riddling. But he couldn't make sense of it, for he also knew about hunting and about the world, and he therefore knew that what they said was *not* true.

The stakes were higher than they might seem. He had either to change his understanding of the world, an understanding that had served him pretty well up to then, or he had to solve the riddle, which would involve changing his understanding of its language, a language he thought he knew pretty well too. Eventually he did solve it, with a little help from the boys. They had been hunting lice, it turned out, body lice on themselves. The lice that they caught and killed they left behind. What escaped them they brought with them. Language put Homer in the dilemma; and language—a word, in fact, the word "lice"—got him out of it. But the dilemma was real. Something had to give: the language or the world. In a riddle it is the language that gives.

It is no wonder that riddles are common across cultures. They celebrate the contradictions we have been talking about, the ones that are central to all stories and songs. "What is like a red, red rose? My love is like a red, red rose." When the Scots poet Robert Burns said this, he was asking us to join him both in a riddle and in a moment of wonder at the strangeness of a world in which love is something it is clearly not. Some people will say that he was fudging, suggesting that one thing is merely "like" another. But the "like" is a foot in the door, or maybe the trickster's hinge that I mentioned in the previous chapter; let it in, let the door swing, and metaphor happens. "My love is a red rose." That's better. It's also stranger. Absolutely true and absolutely untrue all at the same time. Every metaphor contains a riddle, and every good one courts nonsense.

After a while, any metaphor begins to lose its strangeness and to become so familiar that it seems simply true. That's not good; which is what the American writer Gertrude Stein was on about when she said "a rose is a rose is a rose." She was making fun of metaphor, mocking its dedication to strangeness and surprise, and maybe regretting how much it seemed to have lost it.

What is it about strangeness and surprise? From horror movies to stand-up comedians, every generation and every culture seems to have its favourite ceremonies of surprise, and to need them almost as much as it needs ceremonies to calm people down. That's one of the reasons why humour has a hold on us, and perhaps why we pay attention to even the most dismal comedy routine in the desperate hope for some surprise, even if the surprise is one that we (like children listening to nursery rhymes) can see coming for miles.

It is also why we keep coming up with new metaphors, or at least our poets do. William Carlos Williams thought the folks he knew in New Jersey, where he drove the back roads as a country doctor and where there weren't a lot of roses, might need a different sort of surprise, so he said that *his* love was a green glass insulator against a blue sky. He was doing what all good poets do: renewing language, refreshing metaphor, restoring deep contradictions. The poets Michael Ondaatje and Lorna Goodison use cinnamon and onions instead of roses, bringing new surprises, from Sri Lanka and Jamaica, respectively, to the universal language of love. C. S. Lewis once said that the medieval *Romance of the Rose* could not have been written as the *Romance of the Onion*. He may have been right for that particular time and place; but in a wider world, he was wrong.

Strangeness rules story and song. Poets—who profess both—often signal their intention to surprise us right at the beginning of their poems, with lines like "I saw Eternity the other night" (by the seventeenth-century mystic Henry Vaughan), or "I like a look of agony" (Emily Dickinson), or "So much depends upon a red wheelbarrow" (William Carlos Williams). These function in the same way as "Once upon a time," signalling that we are about to cross a border. We don't need to, of course. We can always turn away with a loud *humph*, exasperated by the nonsense of it all. That's what many people did when they first saw Marcel Duchamp's urinal in the art show.

Metaphor is the basic trick of language, and we are sometimes impatient with tricksters. But the door between reality and the imagination can't do without a hinge. "Shall I compare thee to a summer's day?" asks Shakespeare. "Yes," we say; or else we go and do something useful, like washing the dishes. Taking metaphor seriously brings us face to face with the most subversive act of language, since saying A is B undermines our ability—or more important, the ability of language itself—to discriminate between what is true and what is false, what is fact and what is fiction, what is important and what is unimportant.

Linguists used to say that every word was once a metaphor, embodying the wonder of an encounter with something strange; this wonder was then represented in a word, and when the word was repeated, the encounter was experienced again in all its surprising strangeness.

At least that was the theory. The practice turned out to be a little different, for sooner or later words lost this power and degenerated into what Ralph Waldo Emerson used to call "fossil metaphors." The life went out of them . . . until singers and storytellers brought it back, staging new encounters, making old words new again, recovering the wonder of language, and reminding us to believe it and not.

Let's go back to another riddle. Epimenides, an ancient Greek poet and prophet, once said, "Cretans are always liars." But Epimenides was from Crete. Was *he* telling the truth?

The answer, as you might expect by now, is yes and no. If Epimenides is telling the truth—that is, if Cretans always tell lies—then since he is a Cretan, he must be lying. And if he is lying when he says that Cretans are always liars, then since he has just lied he must be telling the truth.

There is a long history to this particular riddle, one that has roots in every tradition of trickery. When Odysseus finally gets home, the stories he tells to trick those who wish him ill conjure up the contradictions of this riddle, for they typically begin, "I am from Crete." But I want to provide a different perspective on this conundrum, and on the tricks that it sponsors. One of the perennial riddles of mathematics has to do with infinity, and one of its best-known illustrations was first posed by the philosopher Zeno a century or so after Epimenides. It contained a contradiction that has haunted storytellers for millennia, and it went something like this. Imagine a runner setting out to run from A to B. First he runs halfway; then half the remaining distance; then half of what's left, and so on, *ad infinitum*. That means he'd have to go an infinite number of steps to cover the distance. In any given amount of time, therefore, he would never arrive. But, of course, we know from experience that he *would* arrive.

What exactly is going on here? This question kept some of the world's best mathematicians and philosophers awake for the next two thousand years. It was sometimes put in the form of a race between Achilles and a tortoise, where the speedy Achilles gives the slowpoke tortoise a head start of half the distance, and then runs twice as fast. He never catches up to the tortoise, according to one impeccable line of logic, and he does catch up, according to another.

The way out of this involves embracing a contradiction at the heart of modern mathematics, which gives us everything from calculus to quantum physics. This contradiction involves not just the riddle of Cretan lies but something called the theory of sets, and a new look at infinity. A Russian genius named Georg Cantor came up with the idea. His achievement has been called the first truly original mathematical innovation since the Greeks, and it was elaborated in a series of papers through the 1870s and 1880s culminating in a great theorem of 1891 with the rather daunting title "The Non-Denumerability of the Continuum." Cantor was a man with a few genuinely nutty ideas, including a conviction that Francis Bacon wrote the plays of Shakespeare and some shadowy information about the British monarchy, which, in his words, "will not fail to terrify the English government as soon as the matter is published." But with his theory of sets he was really on to something.

He began with the simple insight that comparisons, or equivalents, are essential for the measurement of things. Everyone who counts on their fingers knows this, but mathematicians seemed to have forgotten (partly because, as we saw, you *need* to forget in order in order to accommodate negative numbers, irrational numbers and zero). With infinity on his mind, Cantor reminded them. First of all, he said that if we establish a one-to-one correspondence between finite sets, then they have the same number of objects in them—that is, they are "equivalent." He argued that the same was true of sets with an infinite number of objects in them. And then he proved it, after figuring out a way—this was his remarkable accomplishment—of putting such sets into correspondence.

This is the theory of sets. It sounds simple, and in a sense it is. But it has some big surprises. According to it—and I'm jumping through some elegant mathematical hoops here—the number of minutes in all time is the exactly the same as the number of hours, and the number of seconds the same as the number of years. Or if you prefer space over time, the number of points on a line one inch long is exactly the same as the number of points on a line a mile long—or a hundred miles, for that matter. Exactly the same number. The same infinite number. Which is to say, any two lines of different lengths possess the same number of points. So Achilles and the tortoise travel the same distance— even though they don't.

It gets even weirder, but it turns out that this way of thinking is also remarkably workable. It should be; it is very similar to what we do when we tell a story and put ten years into a day (as Homer did) or a day into a novel (as James Joyce did). In a famous passage at the beginning of Laurence Sterne's eighteenth-century novel *Tristam Shandy,* the hero worries that since he has spent two years chronicling the first two days of his life, material will accumulate faster than he can deal with it, and that as the years go by he will be farther and farther from the end of his history. Bertrand Russell picks up the problem, and proposes a solution that is straight out of the theory of sets.

> Now I maintain that, if he had lived for ever, and had not wearied of his task, then, even if his life had continued as eventfully as it began, no part of his biography would have remained unwritten. For consider, the hundredth day will be described in the hundredth year, the thousandth in the thousandth year, and so on. Whatever day we may choose as so far on that he cannot hope to reach it, that day will be described in the corresponding year. Thus any day that may be mentioned will be written up sooner or later, and there-fore no part of the biography will remain permanently unwritten. This paradoxical but perfectly true proposition depends upon the fact that the number of days in all time is no greater than the number of years.

This logic underlies the whole of calculus, which is the way we calculate everything from the speed of a puck to the area of a hockey rink. Calculus involves accepting that Achilles both catches the tortoise and never catches the tortoise. In other words, calculus involves accepting that something both arrives and never arrives, and since that "something" is what calculus calculates, we have a result that both is and is not. True and not true. Sounds like one of those Majorcan stories that begin, "It was, and it was not."

Admittedly, some of the contradictions that emerged from Cantor's theory proved to be very awkward, and preoccupied the next generation of mathematicians. One of the most problematic had to do with what was called the set of all sets. Is such a set a member of itself or not? If it is, it shouldn't be, and if it isn't, it should be. This is the set that Epimenides put himself in.

All of a sudden, Epimenides had lots of company. Bertrand Russell and others spent a good part of their careers puzzling over such paradoxes, and Russell provided another version that became quite popular, about a barber who declared that he would shave all those—and only those—who did not shave themselves. He then realized that he had put himself in an impossible predicament, since if he shaved himself, he shouldn't have, and if he didn't, he should have. There is a large family of riddles like this: "Every rule has an exception," for example. If true, it's false. If false, it's true.

What the mathematicians did—and we may have something to learn from this about the truth value of stories—was to persuade themselves that such contradictions do not lie outside logic but at the centre of it. And so they turned to the axioms according to which logical systems like mathematics operate. One of them, which Cantor relied upon for his theory of sets, was called the axiom of choice. It sounds simple, not to say simple-minded, for it states that if we have a bunch of sets that don't share common elements, then it is possible to create a new set, a "choice" set, consisting of precisely one element from each of the others. For finite sets this process is straightforward. But not for infinite sets; and a number of mathematicians felt that even though the axiom was crucial for set theory, it shouldn't be taken for granted. So they tried to demonstrate that the axiom of choice could be proved from the remainder of the axioms (there were eight others). Then one mathematician, Kurt Gödel, showed that it couldn't be *disproved* from the others; in fact, he showed that *any* system is essentially "incomplete" in this sense. It took another thirty years, and another mathematician by the name of Paul Cohen, to demonstrate that it couldn't be proved from them; not just that *he* couldn't prove it, but that it could *never* be proved. It was independent of them. The cat was out of the bag. It was like saying that the imagination was independent of reality.

But we knew that all the time. Remember those imaginary numbers, and squaring the circle? Couldn't be done, we were told, and then we showed how it could be done by a trick of the magic lantern, a trick of the imagination. Imaginary numbers are numbers that in one sense do not exist—they are independent of reality, or at least of real numbers—and yet we use them all the time.

Indeed, ever since they got serious about imaginary numbers and their independence of real numbers, mathematicians have been on a roll. Euclid's famous parallel postulate (which gives the conditions under which two straight lines will meet) turned out to be independent of the nine others upon which Euclidean geometry was based, and as soon as mathematicians realized this, non-Euclidian geometry became possible—and much of what we now think of as modern science.

My first degree was in mathematics. I loved its patterns and rhythms, its play and its practicality. I loved the way it celebrated the reasonableness of unreasonable things, the seriousness of trivial things, the usefulness of useless things. I loved the "elegance"—a favourite term of mathematicians—of its arguments and proofs. It gave me a new sense of wonder and surprise. And it almost gave me nervous breakdown.

The problem was calculus. It wasn't that I couldn't do it. I just couldn't understand it. It all had to do with the idea of a limit. A limit is anything, a group of racers like Achilles and the tortoise, for example, that converge at a particular point. As ever, nursery rhymes pave the way.

> There was an old crow
>> Sat upon a clod;
> That's the end of my song.
>> That's odd.

This is pure calculus. As we just saw, calculus agrees that Achilles catches the tortoise, even though we don't know how or why. Calculus insists that calculating an *exact* area or *precise* speed can best be done—indeed can only be done—by *approximation*. Put in mathematical terms, calculus accepts that a series of numbers that is approaching a limit (a series like 1, ½, ⅓, ¼, ⅕. . . or 0, ½, ⅔, ¾, ⅘. . .) will eventually, after an infinite number of steps, reach their limit (in these cases, 0 and 1 respectively). Approach is the key word, for the series never actually arrives, precisely because it is an *infinite* series. And yet it does, saying, "That's the end of my song." As the nursery rhyme has it, "That's odd." Though no odder, perhaps, than a jury or judge saying "guilty" or "innocent" at the end of a trial.

Even Isaac Newton, who along with his contemporary Gottfried Leibniz came up with the idea of calculus, stammered when he tried to put it into words, talking about the moment "not before things vanish, nor after, but that with which they vanish." Hardly the clarity we expect of the gentleman who gave us the law of gravity. And yet calculus depends upon our being comfortable with this . . . which is to say, upon our accepting that either/or (either it reaches its limit or it doesn't) is the same as both/and (it both does and doesn't). The limit is both there and not there. It is in a place—infinity, the place of infinite series—where things happen that don't. And this moment, "not before nor after," is a precious, precarious moment of wonder.

It is not surprising that this contradiction caused a lot of confusion and controversy. Bishop George Berkeley, a contemporary of Newton's, turned to mocking those scientists who criticized theology for its unsubstantiated faith. Mathematicians, he rather unkindly pointed out, were building on what seemed to be much weaker foundations. In a satiric book titled *The Analyst, Or a Discourse Addressed to an Infidel Mathematician* (the "infidel" was Edmond Halley, discoverer of the comet that bears his name), Berkeley described Newton's infinite series and their limits as "the velocities of evanescent increments. And what are these same evanescent increments? They are neither finite quantities nor quantities infinitely small, nor yet nothing. May we not call them the ghosts of departed quantities?"

These ghosts of departed quantities, for all the irony in Bishop Berkeley's voice, are the presiding spirits of calculus. My son Geoff, who understands these things, once wrote a story about a fish that didn't like water. Calculus is like that. It lives in the infinite sea and it doesn't like it. It is always looking for dry land, for a place where things have a finite shape and size. But it can't live there, so it dreams about it. If we remember that *dolos,* the original Greek word for a trick, meant baiting a hook for a fish, calculus is the trick that makes it possible for that fish to make its dream come true.

I suggested that mathematical limits focus our attention on the approach rather than the arrival. Prayers work a lot like this too; so do parables, and the godfather of them all, the proverb or aphorism. From folk sayings to philosophical statements, aphorisms have been central to societies for thousands of years. The English word "aphorism" comes from the same root as "horizon," and it used to be said that listening to an aphorism was like walking towards the horizon.

Certainly as a form of story or song, aphorisms (like proverbs) travel well. Typically, they present us with a concise statement or contradiction: "Life is short, art is long" was one of the first (coined by the medical Hippocrates, who published a book of them); or Wilde's "Life imitates art"; or the Christian motto "Service is perfect freedom." They are resolved and then dissolve and are resolved again in an endless sequence of closings and openings. *Ad infinitum*, like Achilles and the tortoise. Aphorisms provide a continual promise of meaning and a continuing disappointment. They are riddles that "tease us out of thought, as doth eternity," in John Keats's image of another endless chase, this one on a Grecian urn where the figures hover between the mortal and the immortal, and between art and life. Aphorisms work like Penelope in *The Odyssey*, weaving the tapestry during the day and unweaving it at night, waiting for Odysseus to get home. Like metaphor, they sustain and subvert the authority of language, and their function, as Ernest Newman (a biographer of Richard Wagner) once remarked, "is really the same as the function of religion—not to be believed."

There is a tale told by the anthropologist Dan Sperber about the Dorze people of Ethiopia. The Dorze are Christians of the ancient Coptic tradition, and they herd livestock, of which the leopard is the most common predator. Now, to the Dorze, the leopard is a Christian animal; this is firmly established in the traditions of their faith. Being a good Christian, a leopard will necessarily respect the fasts of the Coptic Church, which take place on Tuesdays and Wednesdays, for observance of them is a test of faith. But the Dorze still protect their livestock on Tuesdays and Wednesdays. They know that leopards fast on those days, and they know that leopards eat on those days too.

🐾

To close this chapter, I want to go back to riddles and rhymes and another kind of borderline. "Blackheart Man" was one of the early songs of reggae. Written and sung in 1964 by Bunny Wailer, it tells a story about a child being warned by his mother to "take care the blackheart man."

> I say don't go near him
> Take care the blackheart man, children
> For even lions fear him.
> And so the little boy
> can't go here,
> can't go there,
> and ain't supposed to go anywhere. . . .

The blackheart man is the archetypal stranger, living both "in the gullies of the city . . . and the lonely parts of the country." He's mysterious. He's dangerous.

And he's black. Just like Bunny Wailer. It turns out that *this* blackheart man, the one in the song, is as familiar as the face in the mirror, or maybe as the old man clothed all in leather who, in the Richard Scarry book I bought for my children, looked like a cross between our friendly basset hound and their grampa Lew. All of a sudden, Bunny Wailer makes the connection. *He* is the blackheart man, homeless in Babylon, acquainted with grief. He has

> trod the same road of afflictions,
> just like the blackheart man,
> getting his share of humiliation,
> just like the blackheart man. . . .

The blackheart man, the bogey man, the Rastafarian, becomes both the archetypal "man of sorrows" that we met earlier and "the wonder of the city" (as Bunny Wailer calls him), the frightening intruder and the new-found friend. He is the person children know best and have never even seen. He is the ghost under the bed, the stranger they look forward to meeting every night, saying, "How do you do?" He exists only in the stories and songs about him, and he is around every corner. He is pure imagination, keeping reality at bay, and he is rooted in reality, helping us recover the everyday.

But he is strange and scary, dreadfully scary, and he represents the riddle of home, of family, of the familiar, just like that evening prayer I used to say every night represented the riddle of death. It is the riddle of what William Blake called "fearful symmetry," the riddle of creation. Who made the blackheart man? Why do we fight so much? Why is there such suffering in the world?

> Tyger, Tyger, burning bright
> In the forests of the night,
> What immortal hand or eye
> Could frame thy fearful symmetry?
>
> In what distant deeps or skies
> Burnt the fire of thine eyes?
> On what wings dare he aspire?
> What the hand dare seize the fire?
>
> And what shoulder, & what art,
> Could twist the sinews of thy heart?
> And when thy heart began to beat,
> What dread hand? & what dread feet?
>
> What the hammer? what the chain?
> In what furnace was thy brain?
> What the anvil? what dread grasp
> Dare its deadly terrors clasp?

When the stars threw down their spears
And water'd heaven with their tears,
Did he smile his work to see?
Did he who make the Lamb make thee?

Riddles like these are hard to shrug off because their answer presents another riddle, like a set of Chinese boxes or Russian dolls nested inside each other. Except in this case they get larger and larger, rather than smaller and smaller, and their strangeness, like the strangeness of some metaphors, never seems to go away. It is in such riddles that we find faith. Or lose it.

NINE

Charms

IT IS SOMETIMES SAID that poetry begins in riddles and charms, which is to say in the perversity and the power of language. A charm is both magical and musical—the word is related to *carmen,* which means "song"—and it is incorporated into all stories. When we say we live our lives as a tale that is told, we are dealing in charms, as we are when we tell our children nursery rhymes or sing national anthems. Creeds and constitutions are charms, and so are family stories like Teresa Jordan's. They collapse the distinction between the imagination and reality.

One of the first stories I remember had to do with my grandfather John Cowdry. He was standing behind the counter in the little one-room bank that he and his brother had opened a year earlier in Fort Macleod, in the foothills of Alberta. It was 1886. Treaties had just been signed with the Blackfoot, who were expected sooner or later to follow the buffalo into oblivion. Ranching was taking over, turning wooded coulees into cattle wallows. The railroad had arrived in the West. And the Métis leader Louis Riel, who had risen up to defend his people and in doing so nearly brought down the new Dominion of Canada, had just been hanged for treason.

How the Cowdry brothers managed to open a bank still baffles me. The story was that they had spent the previous winter at Pile-of-Bones Creek on the outskirts of Regina, living in a sod house at 40 below, and when spring came, with no money and fewer prospects, they had walked beside a big old ox pulling a Red River cart with all their belongings five hundred miles to the mountains, where warm chinook winds could change the world from winter to summer in half an hour. Like lots of people, they went west for the weather.

They also went for the action. Fort Macleod had been built as the headquarters of the newly established North West Mounted Police, maintaining a peculiarly Canadian kind of law and order that was warped by the commercial concerns of the settlers but worlds away from the violence that disfigured the American West. Just right for someone wanting to go into business. Also, Fort Macleod was a distribution centre for the provisions promised under the Indian treaties, desperately needed in those times of widespread hunger and disease. And it was in the middle of some of the best ranching country. People needed either cash or credit. So John and Nathaniel Cowdry started a bank.

A year later, John was standing with the safe door open, as usual, watching a group of Piegan Indians riding across the edge of town on their way home from south of the border, where they had been trading—some skeptics said stealing— horses. A few cowboys were about, getting supplies before heading north to the Cochrane ranch and round-up. A stranger came into the bank and looked around. There was nobody else there. He pointed a gun at my grandfather. "Hand over the cash," he demanded, "or I'll shoot."

Bank robbers were the stuff of frontier legend, but not yet of Fort Macleod. This one was young—who wasn't in those days?—and what we might call stressed out. My grand-father, who was even younger, was cool and casual. Or so the story goes. He turned around, kicked the safe door shut, spun the handles to set the lock and swung back to face the stranger. "Shoot me and be damned," he said. Then before the stranger could do just that, my grandfather scolded him for his stupidity, and suggested that he should get on his horse and ride out of town before the police came by; then he gave the would-be robber twenty-five dollars out of the counter till to speed him on his way.

That was the story I was told. It had all the elements to catch a child's imagination: danger, heroism and rough hospitality; a stranger heading off into the sunset; Indians just over the hills; a happy ending. And the question of whether to believe it or not. The question of credit. A youngster struggles with it just as much as a banker does.

I certainly believed my grandfather when he told me that story; I was five at the time, and it became for me like a charm. He died shortly after, at the age of ninety, but for the next ten or fifteen years my mother told me the story often. I believed her too, just as I believed my father when he recited "The Cremation of Sam McGee," that old "Song of a Sourdough" by Robert Service.

> And there sat Sam, looking cool and calm,
>   in the heart of the furnace roar;
> And he wore a smile you could see a mile,
>   and he said, "Please close that door."

Just like my grandfather, cool and calm, kicking the safe door shut and saying, "Shoot me." I learned fairy tales and nursery rhymes that way too; and later, Anglican hymns and the national anthem. I listened to them and sang them loudly like a true believer—at least for a moment or two.

Such moments may not last long, but they are like a promise, a covenant, a charm. Recently, I came across another example, part of my grandfather's legacy as well, which broadens the implications of storytelling and gives a new perspective on the borderline between reality and the imagination. It was in the form of a traditional horsemen's quirt, a ceremonial riding crop of Blackfoot heritage about eighteen inches long and two inches wide, in the shape of a small cricket bat. Intricately carved, with a braided leather tail about three feet long and ornamental buffalo hide bound in at the end, it had been in my grandfather's possession since the 1880s.

As part of a BBC documentary on my grandfather's life and times, I took the quirt back to southern Alberta to have it read by experts, both native and non-native. My first reader was an ethnographer at the Glenbow Museum in Calgary, and the quirt told him a story of three successful raids against other tribes, as well as eight scouting and horse-stealing adventures. Along with a gun and a pipe, there were two men represented on the quirt—one probably the owner (carved and coloured in traditional Blackfoot style) and the other representing either all those he had killed in battle or from whom he had taken horses, or else a single famous adversary.

And there were four horses, all finely rendered. Stolen horses. Horse-stealing was very important to many of the plains tribes, part of a deliberate defiance of the kinds of categories and choices that we have been talking about. Horse-stealing was itself a form of storytelling, in fact, celebrating the virtues of thievery and trickery and the value of horses, worthless and priceless all at the same time. The Navajo would have understood this in an instant. The quirt was made when the North West Mounted Police were trying to make horse-stealing a thing of the past, along with Blackfoot stories. The carver of this quirt had something else in mind.

The horses were coloured differently—two were shades of yellow gold, one was red, and the one at the bottom was blue; the Blackfoot have nearly a hundred words for the different colours of horses, but not as many colours in their palette. Two of the horses had reins running down to the ground, signifying that they were especially prized, belonging to a chief or a renowned warrior. They would have been attached by the reins at night to the ankle or wrist of the owner as he slept in his teepee, and the horse thief would have had to have extraordinary skill to steal them, especially in camps in which there would also be fifty or a hundred dogs at any given time. The ethnographer said, with disarming matter-of-factness, that he must have had help. I thought he meant from within the enemy camp; but he was referring to help from the spirits.

The "horse" on the bottom was particularly intriguing, for its ears stood straight up. It turned out that it was not a horse at all, but a mule. Mules were new to the West at that time, brought into the region by the North West Mounted Police, from whom this one would have been stolen.

The ethnographer who read the quirt said he had never seen one quite like this, and suggested that it needed to be read by an elder, ideally in the presence of a ceremonial blanket belonging to one of the great chiefs (and legendary horse-thieves) of the time, Crop-Eared Wolf. He thought the quirt probably belonged to Crop-Eared Wolf himself.

So I went to a town called Stand Off, southeast of Fort Macleod, and arranged to visit an elder of the Kainai (Blood) tribe, wondering whether the account would be different. The elder, Frank Weaselhead, told a story that was precisely the same, matching in every detail the reading of the ethnographer. With one exception. He said that it was the record of a *dream*, not a set of real events; that the story of the dream (which was indeed credited to Crop-Eared Wolf) was still recalled in the tribe; and that it was the dream that brought these remarkable achievements—the raids and horse thefts— to reality. The mule, he said, had appeared to Crop-Eared Wolf to tell him that he would lead any horses he stole across the rivers in spring flood, when horses would typically balk. And the mule had then waited in the closely guarded North West Mounted Police encampment for Crop-Eared Wolf to come and get him. The text was a ceremony of belief, the elder said, not a chronicle of events, and the reading of it was a crucial part of its power, then and now. It was a charm.

I do not know how this quirt came into my grandfather's hands. He had very close associations with the Blackfoot, and it may have been part of a medicine bundle, in which case it belongs back with the Blackfoot to be opened and read again after the first thunder every spring. But the relationship between the dream and the reality that it represents is more common than we might imagine, and belongs to us all through our own stories and songs.

Both these particular stories—about my grandfather John Cowdry and the great warrior and horse thief Crop-Eared Wolf—are charms: one for my family (though it is repeated in histories of the western plains, so maybe it is also for those who want stories like this to make that frontier world into the reality they dream about); and the other for the Blackfoot. Discussing riddles, I said that either language or the world has to give—and in a riddle, language gives. In the two stories I have just told, the world gives, if only a bit. Nonchalance like my grandfather's is too good to be true, even if it is true. And the confidence of Crop-Eared Wolf believing the dream, carving the quirt, and stealing the horses and the mule is too good to be true, even if it is true. That's the whole point of charms.

It is often said that nobody pays attention to anything as unpractical—as dreamy—as poetry any more. I'm not so sure. During the Cultural Revolution, poems were plastered on walls and notice boards everywhere in China, expressions of belief in the power of words to make things happen. And in Poland, during the Solidarity uprising, the fences around the Gdańsk shipyard were covered with poetry. A few years ago, during a program on war poetry, the BBC broadcast a poem titled "Do Not Stand at My Grave and Weep." Its author is unknown; but it had been written down by a soldier in Northern Ireland and left in an envelope for his parents in case he was killed. Within weeks, the BBC received thirty thousand requests for copies. This is the poem, a catalogue of metaphors that stand testimony both to the moving power of poetry and to the ability of listeners and readers to embrace its contradictions and surrender to its charms.

> Do not stand at my grave and weep;
> I am not there. I do not sleep.
> I am a thousand winds that blow.
> I am the diamond glints on snow.
> I am the sunlight on ripened grain.
> I am the gentle autumn rain.
> When you awaken in the morning's hush
> I am the swift uplifting rush
> Of quiet birds in circled flight.
> I am the soft stars that shine at night.
> Do not stand at my grave and cry;
> I am not there. I did not die.

Every time I read this poem I cry, for it brings back very personal memories of loss. It also helps me in ways I cannot explain. Defiance of death is the subject of the poem, though the speaker seems determined to slip out of the struggle and *not* come to terms with death. But rather than convincing us of his demented state (for this is exactly the kind of thing we are told leads to mental illness) the poem opens up for us something else: the possibility of resisting death by embracing it. There is mystery here, in a clarity of metaphors, and there is the intensity of death conveyed with the nonchalance of someone who is still living. It is these contradictions that give us a way to face death, and (when it comes time) to face it down. It is like the mule in Crop-Eared Wolf's dream, carved and painted on his riding quirt: much more than a metaphor and at the same time nothing more than a metaphor, there to lead us through whatever flood of sorrow and suffering we come across.

Elegies are an ancient literary form, maybe the oldest of all; many believe that the earliest poems were epitaphs written on grave markers. Certainly elegies are among the most memorable of the songs we sing, and for a good reason. They set the human imagination up against the overwhelming reality of death, and in so doing they embody both our resistance to it, and our acceptance. This may be why elegies have such a hold on us, from headstones in graveyards to Elton John singing in memory of Lady Diana. Elegies restore the unity of life broken by the experience of death. And yet there is a contradiction here, for in terms of a storyline life has no inevitable conclusion, no immutable plot or pattern or rhythm, *except* death. In death, and in the elegies that commemorate it, the imagination and reality come together in this contradiction, both denying and acknowledging something as certain as the sunset.

From the songs sung at trance dances in the Kalahari or sun dances among the Sioux to canticles in a Christian church or Kaddishes in a Jewish synagogue, this dedication to the power of words to bring comfort and build community is all but universal. For over six hundred years, until early in the twentieth century, the Ottoman Empire was the most significant force in the region stretching from Budapest to Baghdad. At one time or another, its influence extended across North Africa and included most of the Mediterranean coast, the Arab and Jewish communities of the Middle East and the peoples of southern Russia. Along with stories about its formidable military power, the palaces and public buildings are what survive in our imagination. But during those six centuries it was in fact poetry that held pride of place. Almost everybody, from peasant to prince, wrote or aspired to write poetry, displaying a fluency in languages which would be the envy of any literature today and which united, at least in imaginative form, many diverse peoples, across many centuries. Poetry was read and recited on all kinds of occasions, and it entertained and consoled in ways that we would now recognize in everything from crosswords to greeting cards.

Those of us who read poetry in English—and a lot of us do, in one form or another—probably have our favourite lines to keep us company when November comes around. For a long time after it was published in 1751, the most popular poem in the English language was Thomas Gray's "Elegy Written in a Country Churchyard." It is a ceremony of loss, in a language of high formality. "The curfew tolls the knell of parting day," it begins:

> The lowing herd winds slowly o'er the lea,
> The plowman homeward plods his weary way,
>   And leaves the world to darkness and to me. . . .

> The boast of heraldry, the pomp of power,
>   And all that beauty, all that wealth e'er gave,
> Awaits alike the inevitable hour.
>   The paths of glory lead but to the grave. . . .

> Far from the madding crowd's ignoble strife,
>   Their sober wishes never learned to stray;
> Along the cool sequestered vale of life
>   They kept the noiseless tenor of their way.

A century later, it was the lines of the Persian writer Omar Khayyam, who, in an elegant translation by the Englishman Edward Fitzgerald, provided a large number of people with lines to live by. Some of them are still in use.

> Come, fill the Cup, and in the fire of Spring
> Your Winter-garment of Repentance fling:
>   The Bird of Time has but a little way

To flutter—and the Bird is on the Wing. . . .
I sometimes think that never blows so red
The Rose as where some buried Caesar bled;
    That every Hyacinth the Garden wears
Dropt in her lap from some once lovely Head. . . .
The Moving Finger writes; and, having writ,
Moves on: nor all your Piety nor Wit
    Shall lure it back to cancel half a Line
Nor all your Tears wash out a Word of it. . . .

The language of these verses was out of date even at the time they were written, but like the great stories and songs of the Bible, with which they kept company in living rooms and bedrooms, these words caught the imagination of people from all walks of life, people who knew what it was to watch a friend or a community or an entire way of life pass away, or to face death unsure of one's faith, or to lose the hope of love. For my generation, it was the songs of Pete Seeger and Bob Dylan and Joan Baez and Joni Mitchell and . . . everyone will have someone to add. For my children, it might be the songs of U2 and REM and Neil Young and Sarah McLaughlin . . . and even as I write this another name will be on their lips.

The same year as they broadcast "Do Not Stand at My Grave and Weep," the BBC held a poll to discover the nation's one hundred favourite poems. Alfred Tennyson's "The Lady of Shalott" came in second. The winner, by twice as many votes, was Rudyard Kipling's "If."

If you can keep your head when all about you
    Are losing theirs and blaming it on you,
If you can trust yourself when all men doubt you,
    But make allowance for their doubting too;
If you can wait and not be tired by waiting,
    Or being lied about, don't deal in lies,

> Or being hated, don't give way to hating,
>> And yet don't look too good, nor talk too wise. . . .

"Jingoistic rubbish," reacted one newspaper; but the people must have sensed something else. As Griff Rhys Jones (who edited an anthology of these poems) said, "Clearly its sinuous rhythm gets a hold on people who like to get things done." This is a poem for doers rather than dreamers. And it has had more than its share of admirers, from the German Kaiser to Antonio Gramsci, the leader of the Italian Communist party in the 1930s. It was the favourite poem of Marie Stopes, the great advocate of birth control who founded the first clinic in London in 1921 and who obviously found a way of reading it beyond its gendered language. It is still recited by youngsters around the world, and until recently it was the unlikely staple of high-school graduations in Jamaica.

Some would write this last example off as colonial conditioning. But these are the same children who know Bob Marley's lyrics by heart, who would be quick to rise up with Peter Tosh's great chant, "Jah Is My Keeper," and who recite the rough-edged rap of Buju Banton's "Untold Stories," with its classic appeal for dignity, justice and enough to eat.

> I am living while I'm living to the father I will pray
> Only he knows how we get through every day
> With all the hike in the price
> Arm and leg we have to pay
> While our leaders play. . . .

Whatever their age or stage or situation, certain stories and songs seem to hold a place in people's hearts. Different stories and songs for different people, of course, though there are some that seem to move relatively freely across cultures. We need to be as cautious about discounting another generation's songs as we would be about discounting another culture's stories. How can I look down with condescension on my mother and my father, with their carefully folded poems in their purse and pocket which they would bring out and read—or recite by heart—with a mixture of sentimentality and seriousness normally reserved for holy writ? These poems gave them food for their everyday faith.

I remember one of them particularly, by William Ernest Henley. It was called "Invictus," and it was a pre-eminent example of Victorian uplift.

> Out of the night that covers me,
>   Black as the pit from pole to pole,
> I thank whatever gods may be
>   For my unconquerable soul.
>
> In the fell clutch of circumstance
>   I have not winced nor cried aloud.
> Under the bludgeonings of chance
>   My head is bloody, but unbowed.
>
> Beyond this place of wrath and tears
>   Looms but the Horror of the shade,
> And yet the menace of the years
>   Finds and shall find me unafraid.
>
> It matters not how strait the gate,
>   How charged with punishments the scroll,
> I am the master of my fate:
>   I am the captain of my soul.

I didn't know it at the time, but there was a sad story behind these lines. At the time the poem was written, Henley was lying in an Edinburgh hospital, fighting to save his one remaining leg from amputation—he had lost the other when he was six-teen. I used to laugh at the poem's sentimentality, but I guess I should have known better. And I should have understood that its appeal has as much to do with the rhythms and rhymes of the song as it does with the truth of the story. Yeats included it in the *Oxford Book of Modern Verse* that he edited in 1936, and although Yeats was idiosyncratic, he was a poet. More impor-tantly, those lines of Henley's helped a lot of people, just as the songs of Bob Dylan and Bob Marley do. Without wanting to praise too highly, surely we want to leave room for poems and songs that give people courage and comfort.

Are they true or not? Do I care? And do I know what I mean by "true," anyway? These are the oldest questions in human society. And they are, awkwardly, at the centre of many of our current conflicts between Them and Us. We can be clever and postmodern about these questions, but sometimes we want to know.

I suggested earlier that Rastafarianism may be the only genuine myth to have emerged from settlement and slavery in the New World. It is a myth of dispossession and dislocation, of wander-ing and exile, and of home; and it draws on that other great account of racial and religious conflict, seemingly the site of some of the world's most intense antagonism, the Bible. The truth of Rastafari, like the truth of the Bible, is a matter of some moment.

One of the strategies of Rastafari has been to rename things. It's an old trick, as colonizers have realized for cen-turies. I have seen maps of Canada where as many as a dozen different names are layered onto one place, reflecting the dif-ferent traditions of people who have lived there . . . and some-times driven others out. The Rastafarian renaming, too, has involved turning language around so that it reflects their own imaginings and recovers their own realities. "Dread talk," it is sometimes called; with the word "dread" signifying that fearful and fragile wonder that we have met before, in this case exemplified in the power of Jah. The signature "dreadlocks" of Rastafari are a way of catching that mysterious power, or of not losing it, as Sampson did.

Rastafarian dread talk specializes in rhymes and reversals that represent a return to wonder, and perhaps to the surprise of original metaphor. "Oppression" becomes "downpression" (since if you are being pressed down, the pressure cannot be up); "understand" becomes "overstand"; and "site up" means both "see" and "overstand," but always in the further sense of standing up in one's own place. One of the most familiar features of dread talk involves the use of "I," celebrating both the sanctity of the self (as in "I an I" for "we") and respect for Haile Selassie (after a probably deliberate misinterpretation of the Roman numeral I in Haile Selassie I). "I" also sounds like "eye," of course, which is as it should be for the visionary, and like "aye," saying "yes" to Jah rather than simply "no" to Babylon. So "I an I" becomes the signature of Rastafarian revelation and belief. And of what I am calling charm.

In the early 1980s, the elder Ras Kumi wrote down a history of Rastafari. He called it "The Earth Most Strangest Man," and it certainly has a strange quality to it (including some spellings that almost always invite ambiguity). It is a redemption song—a charm—as well as a riddle about home, and I want to quote a bit of it here to suggest that the challenge it presents—the challenge to believe in strangeness—is a familiar one. It is the uncompromising challenge of every riddle, of every metaphor, of every myth, of every religion, of every national story, of everyone everywhere asking for credit. If we can accept its challenge—and I suggest we do so every day in ways we usually don't recognize—then we may be on the way to overstanding the stories and songs of others with whom we may be in conflict. The challenge I am talking about is there in stories and songs of constitutional identity as much as it is in those of cultural expression. If we accept it, we are taken to a place where things happen that don't, where there are ants but not ants, where we celebrate constant sorrow in joyful song. And we'll find ourselves on common ground.

Here is a bit of Ras Kumi's testimonial about the determination of Rastafarians to move back home to Ethiopia.

> I an I live as Sojourners . . . Slaves from Ethiopia always feel deep inside the Spirit of African Movements and move to it in songs.

> Run away Run away Run away
> Haile Selassie I call you
> Bright angels are waiting
> Bright angels are waiting
> To carry the tiding Home
> Blackman. . . .

> I an I get a solace from the words of the Bible. . . . The most important thing about I an I is the way I an I interpret the Bible as Rastafarians. . . . Those in the churches preach that God is the word. I an I accept. In the churches I an I learn that God have many names which he is so called. Yet I an I was only allow to use the name that satisfy the church, yet still there is a doctrine of the church which said my name shall be terrible and dreadful amongst them, I an I chant this chant in this time to fulfill this line:

> A new name you got
> And it terrible amongst them
> The heathen no like your name
> A new Name you got
> And it dreadful amongst them
> The heathen no like your Name.

Such name I an I say Shout it out if you are not a heathen:
RASTAFARI: RAS-Fa-Ta-Ri . . .

I an I is not going to the Promise land that did not coincide
with the text. "In my fathers House there is Many
Mansions. If it were not so I would have told you." To See
Through the glass at the realities of I an I through Law will
enable all people to come forth Representing truth. Then
only then there will be peace.

In many ways, this is a funeral ceremony for the unburied
dead of the Middle Passage and African slavery in the
Americas—the last text is often used in Christian burial services
—but it is also a bringing back of the dead, a ceremony of resurrection, a prayer for peace. And in the face of what he knows
is the skepticism about the Rastafarian dream of home, Ras
Kumi insists that it is *not* a dream, but reality. Furthermore, and
deepening the contradiction, for Ras Kumi Africa is not a
metaphor for home; *home* is a metaphor for Africa. This rever-
sal of the direction of metaphor is vintage Rastafari, and for
Ras Kumi it represents the only kind of imagining that can
resist the grotesque pressure of historical reality. It also provides a way for everyone to believe, precisely because it tests
the limits of faith. Once again it recalls William Blake, for
whom Babylon was a place of the diminished imagination, a
place of spectres, as it is for Ras Kumi; and for whom the only
freedom worthy of the name was to be found in the liberated
and inspired imagination.

When we need this kind of imagining most, of course, is when
we are least aware that we need it at all; when we have made one
of the false choices I have been talking about and find ourselves
overwhelmed or isolated. Usually this happens in ways that are
much less dramatic than the language of being drowned or

marooned would imply. When William Wordsworth said, "The world is too much with us, late and soon,/Getting and spending, we lay waste our powers," he was talking about the everyday world of routine events and manufactured excitements. The social, economic and political imperatives of our societies can be as demanding as anything we will ever encounter, and we often become hypnotized into the delusion that they are permanent and their priorities immutable. Even when we realize that their demands are temporary, they can still be terrible. And when we submit to them we move closer and closer to a life in which we are always under pressure to react to what is happening outside ourselves, or elsewhere, and to surrender to the first thing that offers us any sort of escape.

Two hundred years ago, Wordsworth described this in his own version of the barbaric and the civilized:

> A multitude of causes, unknown to former times, are now acting with a combined force to blunt the discriminating powers of the mind, and unfitting it for all voluntary exertion, to reduce it to a state of almost savage torpor. The most effective of these causes are the great national events which are daily taking place [specifically, the mutiny in the British navy and the impending war with France], and the daily accumulation of men in cities, where the uniformity of their occupations produces a craving for extraordinary incident, which the rapid communication of intelligence hourly gratifies.

War and industrialization, conspiring to herd people into cities and to create a market for cheap distractions, were blunting the spirit and impoverishing the mind. It sounds remarkably familiar; and it is not hard—indeed, it is hard *not*—to see in this a description of our own society. Perhaps the point is that the debilitating pressure of a tedious and at times terrible reality is with us always, everywhere. It is therefore all the more important to turn for sustenance to the treasury of values that stories and songs provide. These values do not inhere in opinions, which may vary, nor in doctrines, which will differ, but in imaginative structures—the rhythms and rhymes of song, the plots and characters of stories, the performances of theatre, the ceremonies of belief. They introduce us to the profoundly human values of friendship, love and loyalty, as well as to the profoundly human conditions of envy, failure and despair. They give a coherence and consistency to human existence that otherwise seems unpredictable and intimidating.

It is only through the pressure of our imagination that we can resist the pressure of reality. This is what charms do. In this sense, all stories are resistance stories and all songs are songs of resistance, pushing back against the tyrannies of the everyday as well as the terrors of the unknown. They give us a way of responding with intelligence and invention when we're confronted with situations and events that are at best incoherent and unstable. Through these stories and songs we discover faith in the possibility of order and significance, and a way to move out into the bewildering world of events without being diminished by it. We recognize the strangeness of reality in the strangeness of our imaginations; and this recognition comes to us in moments of wonder.

All this happens within the traditions of words and images and sounds and movement in the arts and the sciences that together constitute our cultures and give shape and character to our communities. It is these traditions that have permanence, that define what is worthwhile in our lives, and that prevent us from being immobilized by a dumb despair or (what may be worse) mobilized into a blind fury. The only education that matters is the one that teaches us how to watch and listen to them, for it is the ear that is sensitive to sound and rhythm, and the eye that is attentive to pattern and design, that make available their imaginative resources and the nourishment they provide, and that show us how to take comfort in contradiction. For ultimately it is all about the nourishment of what we might as well call the human spirit, that part of us which invents and discovers, as well as listens and watches and waits, and hopes and prays. Without it we are desperate.

Writing about the suffering of Soviets sent to the gulags of Siberia and, closer to home, the suffering of the Cherokee, Chickasaw, Choctaw, Creek and Seminole refugees along the Trail of Tears from their homelands east of the Mississippi to the so-called Indian Territory in the west, Derek Walcott suggested that songs and stories are "the bread that lasts when systems have decayed," passed "from hand to mouth" in times of trouble. This sustenance can come from anywhere, and every community has classics that give it courage and comfort; New Age marketing of Asian and Aboriginal wisdom has left little doubt about that. But we first learn about the power of stories and songs when we are instructed, if not in the classics, at least in the ceremonies of our society at bedtime, or at mealtime, or at play. We learn then and there how to believe, and how to conduct ourselves. Sooner or later, we go further afield and take comfort in other traditions: from the Greeks, maybe, whose stories of men and women and the gods often sound as if they belong in *People* magazine (which we also read for its cautionary tales); or from the descendants of those whom the Greeks called barbaric—the Lebanese singer and storyteller Kahlil Gibran, for example, or the Sufi poet and philosopher "Jalal-ud-Din" Rumi, born in Afghanistan and usually identified as Persian. Many of my generation are more likely to have a copy of one of their books than they are to have the Bible.

I have heard people all around the world say that their most trusted companions are their mothers and grandmothers, or their fathers and grandfathers, who are now dead but with them every day in stories and songs. Plutarch, the Greek historian and philosopher who lived a couple of thousand years ago, said of the people in stories that they were

> friends whose society is extremely agreeable to me; they are of all ages and of every country. . . . Some relate to me the events of past ages, while others reveal to me the secrets of nature. Some teach me how to live, and others how to die. Some by their vivacity drive away my cares and exhilarate my spirit; while others give fortitude to my mind, and teach me the important lesson how to restrain my desires, and to depend wholly on myself.

At the end of the day, this is why stories are at the centre of all societies. An understanding of their power goes deep into our consciousness, and it goes far back in human history.

PART V ❧   *Ceremonies*

of Belief

TEN

Beyond Conflict

STORIES ARE LIKE CURRENCY or lines of credit—which may be two ways of saying the same thing. Credit, after all, means "he or she believes"; and currency demands that we believe the unbelievable . . . that a ten-dollar bill, for example, is worth ten dollars, when we know it isn't worth the paper it is printed on. Currency, like a story or a song, is worthless unless we believe in it—give it a line of credit, as it were.

But exactly *what* is it that we believe in when it comes to a ten-dollar bill? We believe that someone or something "backs," or underwrites, it. For commercial currency, it used to be gold; now it's the government, or the Gross National Product (though the American dollar bill still says "In God We Trust"). In the same way, the credits given by schools and colleges and universities are backed by the institutions themselves.

Who or what backs our stories and songs? Reality or the literary imagination? The history of events or a tradition of performance? There is no single answer; but one thing that will help us get beyond the melodrama of Them and Us is a shared sense of the importance of the question, and of the act of faith that any currency calls for, whether in a piece of paper or the sound of a word.

Gary Holthaus tells about a milking stool his grandfather used on his farm in Iowa. It had only one leg, and most of the day it would lie there, looking broken. It came to life only when his grandfather sat on it, showing a surprising sort of balance that was as sure and graceful as the stool was awkward and uncertain before. Believing in a story is like sitting on a one-legged milking stool. It needs us as much as we need it.

I remember going to a rock concert in Toronto when my daughter Meg was about fourteen. The great Irish group U2 were performing to a large crowd, mostly around her age. These kids seemed to me unlikely material. The group I was shepherding spent the hour or two before U2 arrived on stage going to the bathroom and gossiping. The ones in the row ahead seemed to be trying to start a fight, though fortunately they didn't really have their hearts in it; it was as though they knew that's what you did at rock concerts and wanted to be sure they didn't appear out of place. The kids behind, a bit older, were smoking up, and as the time went by their second-hand smoke offered a kind of relief, a reminder to me of earlier times and places.

U2 arrived, to thunderous applause. I can't recall what they sang as their opening couple of numbers. Like many people, I wasn't paying much attention; in fact, I was preoccupied with trying to figure out why my daughter, MY DAUGHTER, was screaming in such a maniacal way. But then the band began to sing "I Still Haven't Found What I'm Looking For" in a tradition of prayer and lamentation going back thousands of years, opening with drumming that went deep into the soul.

All at once, as though on a signal, the young audience joined in. They knew all the words, and they were there to give voice in a chorus of belief, alone with their private thoughts and in the company of a baseball stadium full of others. For them it was the bread that lasts when systems have decayed—which is to say, when adolescent fears and adult failures tumble down on top of you. Faith itself backed us that evening. That, and the company we kept in singing along.

I have climbed the highest mountain
I have run through the fields

Only to be with you
Only to be with you

I have run, I have crawled
I have scaled these city walls
These city walls
Only to be with you

But I still haven't found what I'm looking for. . . .

I believe in the kingdom come
Then all the colours will bleed into one
Bleed into one
Well, yes I'm still running

You broke the bonds and you
Loosed the chains
Carried the cross
And all my shame
All my shame
You know I believed it

But I still haven't found what I'm looking for.

Why do people sing like that, and what is it that happens when they do? One answer is that it puts them in the presence of a power greater than themselves, although why that would be welcome is anybody's guess. But we do seem to be suckers for it, and for the feeling of being in the grip of overwhelming desire here below and of death hereafter. Not the real thing, of course, but the imagined one, with its promise of a peace that passeth understanding. We share that feeling when we sing in concert. Or is it the other way around? Does singing in concert create the shared feeling?

Whatever the case, there was certainly something magical about fifty thousand people singing together like that. And there was something else. Singing that song, that sad song about unsatisfied desire and soul-longing, everyone seemed full of joy—especially the ones (like me) with tears in their eyes, the ones (like all of us there) who still hadn't found what they were looking for (surely the signature statement of the human condition).

There are all sorts of psychological, sociological, philosophical and political explanations for this. And even literary ones. Edgar Allan Poe once wrote that melancholy is the mood most conducive to great poetry, and then he identified what he called (with his inimitable psychotic flair) "the human thirst for self-torture" as the driving force behind our attraction to many stories and songs—backing them, as it were. Waiting with exquisite anguish for the Raven to say "tomorrow," "soon" or "maybe someday," instead of repeating "nevermore" each time the poet asks his hopeful questions . . . this is what sold more copies of Poe's poem than any other in the nineteenth century and continues to make it popular right through to the twenty-first. As we listen to the litany of questions, we become desperate for another answer, though we know that it will not be forthcoming. And yet we keep wanting, and waiting, and wondering why we bother. The human thirst for self-torture? Or faith? Or something of both?

There is no doubt that this has a lot to do with satisfying our need to find a form for our deepest fears, the ones against which our imaginations struggle. The fears, of course, are real, as real as the terrorism of some latter-day Achilles dragging Hector's body around the town. We hold to stories and songs that chronicle the things we dread precisely because they provide us with some sense of order, with a ceremony of belief in the simple fact of being able to imagine something. But that still doesn't answer the question of what backs them, and why we believe them.

Let's stand back for a moment and look at how stories and songs create this invitation to believe. First of all, as I said about the U2 concert, they put us in the presence of power, and that always fills us with wonder. Stories are always setting people down in the middle of the jungle or the sea or the prairies or the mountains, or setting them up with the forces of love or hate or the conditions of insanity or genius or death. The juxtaposition of the human and the more than human, or the human and the inhuman, is what stories and songs specialize in.

And they are not all that different across cultures around the world. Most of them have to do with relationships: between mass and energy, or between individuals and institutions, or between family expenditures and the GNP, or between the life cycle of a fish and the disposal of chemical wastes, or between the actions of men and women and the history of a nation, or between ogres and ordinary folk. And most of them, across widely different cultures, incorporate a simple vision—of power, or productivity, or causes and effects, or beginnings and ends. The structures of thought and feeling to which they introduce us display a pattern that typically puts one thing, vital and vulnerable at the same time, in the context of something else of larger or more fundamental significance, and then seeks to understand each according to the other. Theology has operated this way from ancient times, but so do the more contemporary logics of the mind and the body, of flora and fauna, of large industries and small businesses. They share not so much a common understanding of the world as a common need to make sense of it.

Stories are not always about people, of course. They are often about things, as in the stories of the natural and physical sciences. They come from a variety of traditions, but their structures—the laws and orderings that shape them—are the product of an imagination that is shared across cultures, including the different cultures of the arts and the sciences. They are most convincing—and most true—when this imaginative scope is recognized. The law of gravitation has only limited interest as a warning about the hazards of sitting under an apple tree. It is much more of a wonder—and it is much more useful as a scientific notion—when perceived as governing the relationship between apples and stars, a relationship that includes in its implications the moon circling about the earth, and the earth about the sun. And although a functional science may teach us both, the habit of mind that is fascinated by relationships between apples and stars, or between King Arthur, the great water and the full moon, is given us by a science that acknowledges its affinities with all the stories that nourish our imaginations.

It is also the habit of mind most likely to maintain a human perspective—a perspective that entertains both the simple pathos of the crippled Arthur and the awe-full majesty of the battle scene, both the earth and the moon and the sun and the stars, both the design of DNA and the determinism of our genetic heritage, both the joy of life and the sorrow of death—or sometimes the other way around. It is this habit of mind, this instinct for wonder, that gives us intimations of order and elegance (which may, of course, include illustrations of mystery and chaos) in all the confusion around. "The most beautiful thing we can experience is the mysterious," said Albert Einstein. "It is the source of all true art and science." So maybe this is why we believe in stories. They are backed by a sense of wonder.

Like the wonder of infinity. I always keep coming back to it, as the place where things happen that don't. "Infinity is in its very nature incomprehensible to us," said Galileo. It is a "disease," said Henri Poincaré, one of the founders of the theory of relativity. "It is only a figure of speech," said Karl Friedrich Gauss, one of the greatest mathematicians of modern times, as he tried to keep his anxiety under control.

They all needed to hear about "not ants, but ants." I talked earlier about the idea of home being almost as bewildering as the idea of a creator. Given the unease about whether infinity was "real" or not, perhaps it was inevitable that one of the most interesting analogies to emerge over the centuries was the analogy between infinity and God, or the gods. Those who thought they might be able to work something out reasoned this way. The line between the finite and the infinite is hard to draw: count as high as you want, "infinitely" high, and you just need to add 1 to keep it finite. The line between the human and the divine is also unclear: the myths of the Greeks, like those of many other great civilizations, are one long attempt to define the difference.

Classical, medieval, and Renaissance scholars all speculated on the ways in which the mathematics of infinity might help draw the line between the human and the divine. Then, in the fifteenth century, one Nicholas of Cusa (or Cusanus, as he was also called) proposed a new definition of God. In doing so, he turned to the most basic elements in geometry: points and lines and curves. Once again, the rational and the irrational went dancing together.

Mathematicians of the time imagined the point in a couple of ways: as the end of a set of lines converging inwards, and as the beginning of the same set of lines directed outwards. Sounds straightforward, but it made the point an image of simultaneous contraction and expansion, or of economy and extravagance. Sort of like the useful and the useless. This was a promising start, for God was praised for both his careful design and his overwhelming abundance.

Cusanus then turned to lines and curves, whose relationship—as we saw with the problem of trying to square the circle—had puzzled people for a long time. He brought the two together in another demonstration of how to do the impossible; in this case, how to turn curves into straight lines. In the imagination, of course.

Cusanus observed that as the distance from the centre of a circle gets larger, the curve of its circumference gets smaller . . . and smaller . . . and smaller . . . until eventually it becomes a straight line, and the circle becomes a square. But we know that's impossible. So Cusanus proposed a logic that would make it possible by imagining that the centre of such a circle must be either everywhere (since the circle is now immeasurably large) or nowhere (since there is no circle). He chose the first as his definition of God. "A centre which is everywhere, but whose circumference is nowhere." It was an image of the infinite that was also an image of the divine. And it helped a lot of people think about both God and geometry by committing themselves to a moment of wonder.

Wonder. For credit, it is as good as gold, and better than most governments.

I think of a story told me by a Yupik woman in Alaska, Martha Demientieff. It was late winter, and one of her closest friends had just died. She was devastated by the loss, unable to say or do anything much at all. At the time, she and her husband, Claude, ran a barge service on the Yukon River, and they needed to get ready for the coming season. But she couldn't even get ready for the coming day. One morning she lay down on one of the barges. The ice was just starting to melt, and she heard the groaning sound it makes as it begins to break up and loosen its hold on the river. The groans surrounded her as she lay there on the barge, both of them still bound tightly in the iron grip of winter. It was the sound of a struggle coming from deep within the season, and within her soul, and it seemed that she and the barge and the river were one in their agony. Then slowly the groaning gave way to a fierce crashing, as huge chunks of ice smashed against each other and against the barge. One struggle had turned into another, louder this time but with a promise of movement, of an opening, of spring. The noise was overwhelming now, like being in the middle of a giant ice crusher, and then suddenly, as though by some kind of grace, the struggle was over. The chunks broke up into small bits. A sound like the tinkling of small bells came to her ears. The river was back, and Martha too. She turned those sounds into a story that gave form to her grief and a way to talk about it.

How this happens, how a kind of joy comes out of a song of sorrow, is one of the mysteries of art, as baffling as any of the mysteries of science. It requires, and rewards, faith. Understanding it is part of understanding how stories work, how they offer a moment in which the imagination pushes back against reality even as it surrenders to it. It is a covenant in wonder between ourselves and the world. It could be the wonder of horses, or of home. Here it is more like the wonder that we all felt singing "I Still Haven't Found What I'm Looking For."

The final piece of the puzzle has to do with where that wonder comes from. That's when we need to know about the different ways stories work. What may at first seem like a tangent will, I hope, put us on the way to an answer. Let's return to Wordsworth, and his poem about daffodils. Here's the first stanza.

> I wandered lonely as a cloud
> That floats on high o'er vales and hills,
> When all at once I saw a crowd,
> A host, of dancing daffodils;
> Beside the lake, beneath the trees,
> Fluttering and dancing in the breeze. . . .

These days many people don't much like this poem because it is too precious. In Wordsworth's day, readers didn't much like it because it seemed so common. Indeed, of all the poets of his time, Wordsworth was the one most often identified with the yard rather than the tower. He used its language, the language of the ordinary men and women of his native Northumbria; and he wrote more about its people—including its beggars and gypsies and mad women and idiot boys—than any major poet in English in the previous two hundred years. And, of course, he wrote about daffodils. Nobody wrote about daffodils in Wordsworth's time, except Wordsworth. Daffodils were ordinary flowers, yard flowers. Not your tower types, like roses. Not tame flowers, garden flowers, but flowers that grew wild, flowers you would see when you were wandering about. He even began his most famous collection of poems, the one with all his great sonnets in it about the struggles for liberty of the English and the French and the Scots and the Swiss and the Swedes and the Haitians, with a poem about an even more common roadside flower, the daisy . . . and then he added two more poems about daisies later in the collection.

How can a poet write a proper poem about an improper flower? the critics asked. It's like having a ceremony to celebrate barbarism. Even more to the point, how can a poet do it when revolution is abroad? This was the time of the American and French revolutions, after all, and England itself was seething with unrest. To bring this up to date, how can a poet write anything at all when people are dying in the streets, the countryside is ravaged by pollution, and there is work to be done to make the world a better place? In a poem titled "Cold Comfort," the Jamaican poet Edward Baugh describes how, after reading the poem "Aubade" by Philip Larkin, he had

> the authentic shivers, gooseflesh.
> Then started worrying about how
> supposedly death poems and
> love poems are luxuries
> we in the third world
> cannot afford.

But as Baugh implies, poetry is a luxury in the way that falling in love is a luxury—the way moments of peace and hope are luxuries in a life of trouble and despair. The way lying on a barge on the Yukon River on an early spring day is a luxury for a native woman overwhelmed by grief and with work to do.

A story's subject neither guarantees nor compromises its credibility. This is both the strangest and the most comforting thing of all, for it gives hope of finding common ground in ceremonies of belief that do not necessarily share the same subject. The fact is that the wonders of the mind and spirit, which *are* shared, are always implicated in the workings of the everyday. As the Uruguayan writer Eduardo Galeano insisted in an essay nicely titled "The Imagination and the Will to Change":

> The literature that is most political, most deeply committed to the political process of change, can be the one that least needs to name its politics, in the same sense that the crudest political violence is not necessarily demonstrated by bombs and gunshots. . . .
>
> Those who approach the people as if they were hard of hearing and incapable of imagination confirm the image of them cultivated by their oppressors. . . . Literature that shrinks the soul instead of expanding it, as much as it might call itself militant, objectively speaking is serving a social order, which daily nibbles away at the variety and richness of the human condition. . . . I believe that literature can recover a political, revolutionary path every time it contributes to the revelation of reality. . . . From this point of view, a love poem can be more fertile than a novel dealing with the exploitation of miners in the tin mines or workers on the banana plantations.

Sometimes the relationship between the personal and the political takes a different form, recalling an old opposition between what used to be called particulars and universals. The debate about them goes back a long way in European thought—back to Boethius, in prison near Milan in the year A.D. 525 in the dark end-days of the Roman Empire, writing a medieval bestseller called *The Consolation of Philosophy*. But it isn't some dusty old issue; on the contrary, it is around us constantly. It is there in the arguments about standards determined here or elsewhere; about advice coming from those directly involved or those distant and detached; about local speech and literary writing. It is there in the contradictions between individual and collective rights, and between local laws and those of supposedly higher standing. Civil disobedience rests its case upon this distinction, which received eloquent expression in Martin Luther King Jr.'s "Letter from Birmingham Jail" when he answered charges that his actions were untimely, that he was an outsider, and that he was disobeying a particular law of the land with an appeal to the universals of justice and freedom. And it is there in the continuing discussion about whether our stories and songs—especially those we teach at home and through the collective enterprise of our schools and universities—should be located in ordinary experiences, or set above and beyond them. The yard and the tower once again.

Choosing between them is foolish, as we have seen—and ultimately impossible. But the distinction is there to be recognized. Some stories derive their credibility from real places, and we value them for that; others are located on what the Greeks used to call Parnassus, an ideal place well away from the everyday, which gives such stories their own kind of importance. People have often pointed out the shortcomings of each place and each point of view, usually with considerable passion. An exclusive commitment to particulars—that is, to real situations or what I have been calling the yard—limits us to a diminished perspective and precludes any genuine understanding of the world as a whole, the argument goes. Life in the

tower, on the other hand, leaves us caught up in absurd gener-
alizations and completely detached from life. This can all be
turned around, of course: the tower, especially if it doesn't
have any windows, quickly becomes a place of isolated particulars; and the yard, if it doesn't have walls, encourages incoherent universals. That's why we have such trouble dealing
with religious fundamentalists: we're never quite sure whether
they are locked in the tower or loose in the yard.

The power of stories does not depend on whether they
are located in the yard or the tower. It depends on where they are
located in relation to the forces that fill us with wonder, and
sometimes dread. That is why literary canons cause so much
controversy. And yet it is not so much the individual stories
themselves as our insufficient understanding of how they work
and why we give them such currency that causes most of the
trouble as we try to find common ground. Jonathan Swift—
who was Irish, and knew all about these things—once wrote:
"We have just enough religion to make us hate, but not enough
to make us love one another." This happens when we misunderstand how stories get their power.

Stories tend to one of two basic models: either they describe
stages and sequences, causes and effects; or they tell how things
and events fulfil an overall purpose and design. The first are
interested in beginnings and processes; the second in endings
and products.

Most stories shuttle between. This is especially obvious in
stories of religion. They are always more or less about the
greater design of things, their universal purpose or end; but they
often illustrate this by telling us about the means, the mechanisms, the particular good or evil. Science is always confusing
them too; stories about stages and sequences conjure up considerations of larger purposes and overall design. When Charles
Darwin tried to extricate his theory of evolution—which was all

about process—from the image of natural selection—which implied a selector picking a product which would guarantee the survival of the fittest—he complained: "It has been said that I speak of the natural selection as an active power or deity; but who objects to an author speaking of the attraction of gravity as ruling the movement of the planets? Everyone knows what is meant and is implied by such metaphorical expressions, and they are almost necessary for brevity."

Well, if everyone knows, they seem to forget. And not only are they encouraged to do so by phrases like "natural selection" or "the law of gravity," it is correct to confuse the two. The theory of evolution is about the complex relationships between heredity and the environment, nature and nurture. So is the story of the creation of the world in any of a hundred different cultures, where the motivation of the creator is constantly implicated in the conditions of the world, and where the stages of creation are bound up with the strategy of the creator.

But still, there *is* a difference. Let me take this a little further, with some help from one of the greatest biologists of the twentieth century, D'Arcy Thompson. His name has all but disappeared behind that of people like Richard Dawkins and Stephen Jay Gould, who have helped many of my generation understand the mysteries of the natural world; but D'Arcy Thompson's book *On Growth and Form*, which first came out in 1917, was a landmark study of the relationships between these two fundamentally different but inextricably linked modes of explanation. Here is Thompson himself, writing out of his training as both a classicist and a scientist:

> Time out of mind it has been by way of the "final cause,"
> by the teleological concept of end, of purpose or of
> "design," in one of its many forms (for its moods are
> many), that men have been chiefly wont to explain the phe-
> nomena of the living world, and it will be so while men

have eyes to see and ears to hear withal. With Galen, as with
Aristotle, it was the physicist's way; with John Ray, as
with Aristotle, it was the naturalist's way; with Kant, as with
Aristotle, it was the philosopher's way. It was the old
Hebrew way, and has its splendid setting in the story that
God made "every plant of the field before it was in the
earth, and every herb of the field before it grew." It is a
common way, and a great way, for it brings with it a glimpse
of a great vision, and it lies deep as the love of nature in the
hearts of men . . . liken[ing] the course of organic evolution
not to the straggling branches of a tree, but to the building
of a temple, divinely planned, and the crowning of it with
its polished minarets. . . .

But the use of the teleological principle is but one way,
not the whole or the only way, by which we may seek to
learn how things came to be, and to take their places in the
harmonious complexity of the world. To seek not for ends
but for antecedents is the way of the physicist, who finds
"causes" in what he has learned to recognize as fundamental properties, or inseparable concomitants, or unchanging
laws, of matter and energy. In Aristotle's parable, the house
is there that men may live in it; but it is also there because
the builders have laid one stone upon another. It is as a
mechanism, or a mechanical construction, that the physicist
looks upon the world, and Democritus, first of physicists
and one of the greatest of the Greeks, chose to refer all natural phenomena to mechanism and set the final cause aside.

Still, all the while, like warp and woof, mechanism and
teleology are interwoven together, and we must not cleave to
the one nor despise the other; for their union is rooted in the
very nature of totality. We may grow shy or weary of looking to a final cause for an explanation of our phenomena; but
after we have accounted for these on the plainest principles of
mechanical causation it may be useful and appropriate to see

how the final cause would tally with the other, and lead
towards the same conclusion. . . . The philosopher neither
minimizes nor unduly magnifies the mechanical aspects
of the Cosmos; nor need the naturalist either exaggerate or
belittle the mechanical phenomena which are profoundly
associated with life, and inseparable from our understanding of growth and form.

With this all-inclusive perspective in mind, we may find it
much easier to reconcile conflicting creation stories, or stories
of conflicting covenants to land. Darwin's theory of evolution,
for all its mechanisms, became increasingly associated with a
purposefulness in which (in Thompson's words) "every variety of form and colour was urgently and absolutely called
upon to produce its title to existence either as an active useful
agent, or as a survival of such usefulness in the past." This is
where it ran head-on into the Bible. But it represented a purposefulness without an ultimate purpose, an adaptation without a design (other than to produce precisely that form or
colour). And this allowed room for both Genesis and genetics.

There is one other arena of storytelling we need to look at. It
has to do with the different ways we think about society itself.
This difference may be the one that causes more trouble than
any other. It is also older than any other.

First of all, there is the notion that communities—from the
neighbourhood to the nation—are humanity's most ingenious
inventions, the most *convenient* form of human organization.
On the other hand, there is the idea that they constitute the first
and natural form, the *inevitable* form. The difference here
between the artificial and the natural, or the organized and the
organic, has given rise to two ideas about human society.

One holds that any society or group is made up of con-
stituent parts, which contribute to the whole in a more or less

complicated way. Without its parts, the whole would not exist; with them, it becomes something that is different from (and usually greater than) the sum of its parts. This idea underlies the ideology of liberal individualism, in which the individual, rather than the group, is the focus of moral and political attitudes, and the community or state is admired primarily for the ways in which it provides opportunity for the exercise of individual liberties. It is a necessary convenience, embodying a contract or fulfilling a design and existing to serve and protect individual interests.

If we take the alternative idea, then we accept that the larger social entity is not one to which we (however theoretically) elect to belong but within which we find ourselves, willy-nilly. The society or state is a natural organic form rather than the product of ingenious artifice. Instead of the individual existing prior to the state and giving it whatever larger significance it has, the individual receives life and meaning *from* the state, much as a branch does from the tree.

In the first model, individuality is valued above all else, and group identity is celebrated only insofar as it enhances this. Most democracies are more or less dedicated to this idea. The second presumes that individuality derives from and depends upon belonging to a group, and it celebrates the social group as a natural and inevitable family of interests rather than an artificial and convenient one. With its belief in the natural priority of the group, it provides a political philosophy for those who find themselves born into a community with a strong territorial or religious or racial identity, of which the tribe or nation often represents the most significant expression.

These two ideas have complemented and contradicted each other for millennia. They sometimes take the form of a classic conflict between determinism and free will: we are who we are because we behave that way, or because we are born that way. This difference shapes the response of people from different societies to their foundational myths. Some of them are celebrated because of the ingenious explanation they provide, while others are accepted with the same sense of inevitability as family. And yet it is not a question of choosing between them, for if we listen carefully, we will recognize their interdependence.

But often we *don't* listen, and extend the distinction into new definitions of difference. And so people say that Western—by which they usually mean European—views of time are linear, while those of other peoples are circular. This is nonsense, but it's stubborn nonsense. Most of the stories we hold dear, in the sciences as well as the arts, display elements of both. We negotiate time's "arrow" and time's "cycle" constantly in all cultures, holding together the notions of time as an irreversible linear succession of unrepeatable events (the passing of the hours, the flow of a river, the end of a century) and as the cyclical agency of fundamental and continuing states (the turn of the century, the cycles of the moon, the corn festival and Yom Kippur and Christmas). Unless we pay attention to the constant negotiation between them *within* cultures, we end up dividing the world into those who think in linear terms and those who do not.

Such distinctions are at best misguided; and at worst, they create conflicts that are dependent on choices that we should not be making. More and more, we seem to be offered alternatives that encourage us to identify essential differences between cultures. Take the example of aboriginal scientific inquiry provided by the Sioux historian Vine Deloria Jr.

> If we were to raise a herd of buffalo on an exceedingly large tract of land we might one day discover we did not know where they were. Turning to western science we would scamper through reports on buffalo behaviour, we would get a map and try to pinpoint the location of streams

and watering places and we might organize a search for the herd. . . .

In addition to everything that we can reasonably determine as valid data in locating the buffalo, however, the tribal tradition has a few additional bits of information that would make our task easier.

The buffalo loved sunflowers. At times they would gather in a draw where the sunflowers grew and frolic among them, uprooting the plants and tossing them over their heads onto their backs so that they were virtually decorated with these colourful flowers. So we might look more closely at sunflower patches. Grazing buffalo frequently had flocks of blackbirds among them. The birds would sit on the backs of the buffalo and when the animals grazed and disrupted the insects, the insects would give themselves away, making them easy prey for the birds. We would then narrow our search to locations with sunflowers and many blackbirds. If we were really sophisticated we would know that on top of many of the buttes and hills on the northern plains lives a little dun beetle that has two antennas on its head. These antennas *always* point to the nearest buffalo herd, whether that herd is down in the next valley or fifty miles away. All we need do is pack a picnic lunch and move from one group of beetles to another until we locate the herd. . . .

Some facts might have come from dreams, others from communication with beetles, and other facts from knowledge of birds, which would include their relationship with the buffalo. This information is not extraneous to the knowledge of buffalo and it is not simply an ad-hoc observation. It is included in the teachings of the tribe regarding these animals. And it can be used to predict buffalo, bird, insect and flower behaviour. Within the western scientific framework . . . it would be exceedingly difficult, if not impossible, to discover these kinds of relationships.

He is right, of course. But not for the reasons he proposes. Thinking in analogies goes back a long way in every society, and it cuts across the arts and the sciences precisely
because it is bound up in how language and the imagination
work. Deloria's account, while it demonstrates the strategies
of one particular aboriginal science, also displays similarities
with other scientific models. Both so-called Western science
and that of the Sioux maintain a continuing allegiance to both
reality and the imagination, and they converge precisely at
the point where they each embrace the figurative as the fac-
tual. Western science is most literal when it is most figurative. A mathematical equation is pure metaphor, pure song
and pure story. $x^2 + y^2 = r^2$: that's a circle. $e = mc^2$: that's
relativity.

Furthermore, what Deloria is describing has been a key
element of Western thought from Aristotle on, and probably
long before. It displays the importance of relationships
between things apparently disconnected, or the "similitude in
things to common view unlike," as the astronomer Johannes
Kepler once said. It informs all metaphor, of course, and it is
also what creates that connection between apples and stars
which gives the law of gravity its enormous power. To say that
it is an exclusive characteristic of native American science is to
misunderstand the nature of all science, and all stories. Newton
did not show the cause of the apple falling. He showed a relationship between earthly and heavenly bodies. The "final
cause" of gravity remains one of those mysteries Einstein
talked about. And so does the final cause of the marvellous
interdependence that Deloria describes.

Writing at the end of the nineteenth century, at a time when
science and religion were at war, the scientist J. B. S. Haldane
made an interesting distinction. Religion, he suggested, is a
way of life and an attitude to the universe. It brings us "into
closer touch with the inner nature of reality. Statements of

fact made in its name are untrue in detail, but often contain truth at their core. Science is also a way of life and an attitude to the universe. It is concerned with everything but the nature of reality. Statements of fact made in its name are generally right in detail, but can only reveal the form, and not the real nature of existence."

With this in mind, it is time to look at how ceremonies of belief offer a way beyond conflicts between cultures—including the cultures of religion and science—and a way of reimagining Them and Us.

ELEVEN

Ceremonies

THE GITKSAN PEOPLE of the northwest of British Columbia have lived in the mountains, fishing and hunting and farming and trading, for thousands of years. They have a story that tells of changes to one of the river valleys, near the mountain called Stekyooden, across from the village of Temlaxam. It was once the centre of their world, one of those places that bring peace and prosperity to the people who live there.

This valley nourished the Gitksan people so well that they became unmindful of their good fortune and forgot the ways that the mountains and the rivers and the plants and the animals had taught them. The spirit of the valley, a grizzly bear called Mediik who lived by Stekyooden, warned them and gave them many signs of his anger, but they ignored these warnings. Finally Mediik got so angry that he came roaring down from the top of the mountain. Grizzlies running uphill are breathtakingly fast; I've been chased by one, and he looked like a freight train impersonating a gazelle. But because their front legs are short, grizzlies sometimes slide or tumble coming downhill, and Mediik brought half the mountain with him, covering the valley floor and the village of Temlaxam and all the people there. Only a few survived, those who were out hunting in the high country or berry picking on the opposite slopes or doing the hard work that makes for an easy life.

This was just about seven thousand years ago. Over time, the people returned to the valley; and although never the rich and fertile home it once had been, it always held its place in their history and they remember the great grizzly and the lesson he taught them. Today the stories of the Gitksan move out from that valley like spokes from the hub of a wheel or children from their parents. It is the centre of their lives, the place they came from, and the place to which they return their thoughts and their thanks. Their present-day claims to the territory arise from the claims that the valley has on them, and the story of the grizzly and the slide confirms both claims.

Several years ago, when the Gitksan decided to assert their claims in the courts of the newcomers to the valley, they told this story. They told it with all the ritual that it required, for as Mary Johnson reminded the court, the stories and songs that represent their past are about belief, and therefore need ceremony.

So do all stories, the Gitksan realized. They also realized that the story of the grizzly and the sacred mountain called Stekyooden and the village of Temlaxam, which in their minds confirmed the presence of their people in that place for millennia, might not be believed by the judge, schooled as he was in stories of a different sort. So one of their leaders, Neil Sterritt, suggested they draw on another storyline to complement their own. They had geologists drill under the river that still runs through the valley and take a core sample and analyze it. A scientific ceremony. They discovered that sixty feet down there was clay that matched the clay high up on the mountain slope, exposed where the grizzly had taken down the hillside—or where the earthquake had produced the slide that brought down half the mountain. And the sample was dated exactly when their story said the grizzly grew angry with the people in the valley, seven thousand years ago.

The court was inclined to see the scientific story as confirming the legendary one. However, the elders of the Gitksan were at pains to persuade the judge that each story was validated by the other; that neither had a monopoly on understanding what happened; that the storyline of geology was framed by a narrative just as much the product of invention as the story told by their people; and that each storyteller's imagination—whether telling of tectonic plates or of grizzly outrage—was engaged with discovering a reality that included much more than the merely human.

The story of the grizzly is a very old one, hardened on an anvil of ancient tellings and tested by memories that disputed it for much longer than our seismic and sedimentary theories. The Gitksan believe both of them. Both, for them, are true. Bear and *bear*, as it were. Both help their people live their lives. And both are revealed in stories.

The Mediik story may seem familiar to many of us, of course, because it is the story of a flood—*the* flood, for the Gitksan. But its power comes not from that connection, nor from the fact that flood stories are common across cultures, but from the way it complements a scientific account, insisting on its own authority without discrediting the other. Believe it and not.

The notion of contradictory truths is troubling, but well beyond a setting sun and a round earth we routinely accept all sorts of them. Think of two painters sitting early one evening across the harbour from a ship at anchor. One of them, working in one mode of truthtelling, paints the ship according to the knowledge that she has of it—for instance, that it has twenty-seven portholes and is grey. The other, working in an equally creditable tradition, paints seven portholes, because that's all he can see in the twilight, and he paints the ship in unlikely tones of pink and green, because that's what it looks like from where's he's sitting at that hour of the day. He knows it's wrong, but he also knows it's right. The so-called Impressionists in the nineteenth century, who were sticklers for truth as they saw it—even when what they saw was a pink cathedral—used to call this "seeing with an innocent eye," a perception undirected—unsocialized might be the current term—by painterly conventions and viewer expectations.

Which is the true portrait? Both are determined as much by conventions of style as they are by any certainties, and either, taken out of its frame of reference, can be made to seem false or foolish. On the other hand, both are believable; and we can believe both, praising each for its authenticity and authority.

Every imaginative tradition has allegiances both to the facts of experience, which in a sense are part of us, and to the formalities of expression, which are separate from us. To life and to art, we might say. Two truths? Perhaps; but instead of two truths we might say two stories, which together help us chart the convergence of reality and the imagination, showing us how conventions of storytelling or painting or science or religion are best understood not in isolation but by seeing where they meet others, and the world, in ceremonies of belief—ceremonies underwritten by the kind of faith John Polanyi talks about when he says that it is the incredible belief that there exists a grand design underlying the physical world which makes scientists dedicate their lives to science.

Earlier, I mentioned borders. I think the problem with poems and paintings and performances from other cultures is not their strangeness, which some part of us always welcomes, but the way in which they give a signal that we are at the border. Often we miss it. And that's a problem. In theatre, the stage itself provides that signal—perhaps the reason theatre travels well. But in stories and songs we sometimes mistake one kind of signal for another, and either cross the border inadvertently or never get there. In the first case we miss the moment of wonder, of contradiction, and become overwhelmed by reality. In the second, we remain like Achilles and the tortoise, isolated in the imagination.

When I was working in Belfast in the 1980s, both Catholics and Protestants set borders by means of slogans chalked on the walls of buildings. Usually they were warnings, sometimes crude (like "Fuck the Pope") and sometimes coded (like "Greater love hath no man," which were supposed to be the last words of Bobby Sands, the IRA fighter who died during a hunger strike). It was deadly dangerous to misinterpret the message, and you certainly did not linger on the borderline. But then there appeared a haunting riddle: "Is there a life before death?" It was written up in no man's land; and whenever it was wiped off at night it would appear again the next morning, signalling common ground on which everyone could meet. On the border between sense and nonsense.

This border is where strangeness disappears and then reappears again in a new guise. It is where we stay in any good story or song. Crossing the border is like going up onto the stage and saying, "This isn't Hamlet; it's Laurence Olivier"; or "There aren't really any red ants." We attack the very strangeness and contradiction we should cherish. Not getting to the border is to mistake the imagined events on stage for real life—becoming locked into its imaginary world—and yell out to Desdemona that Othello is going to kill her, or to watch out for those red ants. We avoid the contradiction and strangeness.

Our failure to recognize the border may be the singer's or storyteller's fault as much as our own. But even if it is not always easy to be sure where the borderline is, there are usually clues. The most reliable have to do with the moment that Martha Demientieff described when the line between ice and water, winter and summer, joy and sorrow disappears, and so does the line between "yours" and "mine." It is the moment when mystery and clarity converge, when we cannot tell whether we have surrendered ourselves or are still separate, when intensity has a casual quality to it. We don't always hear tinkling bells, as Martha Demientieff did, but we know the feeling from early in our lives, and once we have recognized it in our own culture we can identify it in others. That's the beginning of moving beyond Them and Us. It's not that there's no difference, any more than we would say there's no difference between reality and the imagination, or between the useful and the useless. Of course there is. But the difference becomes transformed in the ceremony of belief that is the story. Funeral ceremonies provide an illustration of this, reminding us of loss even as they restore our sense of community, completing the circle even as they remind us that it can be broken. We need to understand that it is in the act of believing in these stories and ceremonies rather than in the particular belief itself that we come together, and that this act of believing can provide the common ground across cultures that we long for. We need to understand because our lives depend upon it.

It is an ancient conviction that if this doesn't happen properly it doesn't happen at all.

> When names are not used properly, language will not be used effectively; when language is not used effectively, matters will not be taken care of; when matters are not taken care of, the observance of ritual propriety and the playing of music do not flourish; when ritual propriety and the playing of music do not flourish, the application of laws and punishments is not on the mark; when the application of laws and punishments is not on the mark, the people will not know what to do with themselves.

This is Confucius, in *The Analects;* and what he is calling for is discipline and ceremony in the use of language. For all its unfamiliar connections and antique decorum, his injunction informs a great deal of what we do in our schools and colleges and universities. We teach correct names—in particle physics, plant biology, human physiology, property law, pharmacy, prosody; and we try to show how everything follows from that. This is what the disciplines and the decorums of all cultures are about, and it is why we emphasize the need for correctness: in the languages of the arts and sciences; the logics of disease and the decline of empires; the litanies of religious faiths and regulatory regimes. Of course, every now and then the standards change, and a new kind of correctness comes into play; but it has to prove itself against the old correctness, and it has to overcome what Northrop Frye once called "the majestic power of inertia, the greatest of all political forces."

All ceremonies offer the possibility of understanding the nature of belief and the correctness of names, especially when the ceremonies are strange to us . . . and in some measure they always are if we let them be. "This is my body," says the priest in a ceremony of Christian communion, holding a wafer and quoting Jesus at the Last Supper. Then he eats it, and asks us to do the same. These are *very* strange table manners.

Anyone who takes this form of the Christian communion seriously believes that the wafer and the wine at the very least "stand for" the body and the blood of Christ. There's that foot in the door again. Some even believe that the wafer and the wine, at least for the moment of communion, *are* the body and the blood. Theologians call it transubstantiation. Literary critics call it metaphor. We might as well call it a contradiction. And a pretty unnerving one at that.

Yet we often seem remarkably comfortable with it. Not necessarily with the communion service, of course, though lots of people the world over believe in something like this within their various religions. But even those who do not, those who are unlikely to believe in things such as transubstantiation, routinely repeat the creed of some faith or other in defiance of the very dubious things that it contains and the doubt that is in their hearts. I mean no disrespect by this; for at the moment of saying so, they *do* believe. And properly so.

There's something else that's odd here. These moments of confession and contradiction are usually communal. With witnesses, that is. Now why on earth would we want to say such questionable things where others can hear us? A rock concert is only one of many such occasions. When we sing our national anthems, we use words and phrases about people and places that we would almost certainly question in any other context. We say we believe when maybe we really don't . . . except right at that moment, the ceremonial moment, when we reach the border.

There are no ceremonies more important to the imagining of individual and collective identity, and no agreements more bound up with misconceptions about civilians and barbarians, than our contracts with each other. War and peace treaties set the limits, and between them we have all sorts of arrangements determining how each of Us will be engaged with Them. Sometimes these take the form of political constitutions; sometimes Biblical covenants; sometimes mutual commitments to do something, like reduce greenhouse gases, or not to do something, like kill whales. They give communities a sense both of obligation and entitlement. Singing songs together, sitting down together, agreeing to set aside this place as sacred, acknowledging that place as special.

Often, like table manners, these contracts and covenants seem silly to those of us who are not bound by them in belief. But like other nonsense—riddles and charms come immediately to mind—we need to recognize their claim on people's hearts and minds. Respect due, as Rastafarians say. Whatever form they take, such ceremonies are all more or less about culture and anarchy, or the civilized and the barbaric.

Few have been more problematic than the treaties entered into between aboriginal peoples and settler societies, which in their range represent every international agreement we have between people who have moved onto land and those who claim it as their home. And sadly, we have a lot of these. Understanding more about these treaties might help us understand how we can answer the question "If this is your land, where are your stories?"

I think one answer goes like this. Well, we've got *two* stories: one is a chronicle of events, how we came to be here; and the other is a ceremony of belief, why we belong here. Both are true, the way both of those paintings are true; but if we try to compare them we run into trouble, and end up dismissing one or the other as untrue.

Our two stories are probably matched by a couple of stories that you have. Let's see if we can put our stories beside each other, the way we did with the grizzly's mudslide and the geologist's core sample, and identify the ones that are about branching trees and the ones that are about building homes, the ones that are about patterns and the ones that are about purposes, the ones that go in circles and the ones that go in straight lines.

Maybe then we will understand that all too often we try to match the unmatchable, such as what J. B. S. Haldane called statements of fact that are untrue in detail but contain truth at their core with those that are right in detail but only reveal the form and not the real nature of things. This is a sure recipe for misunderstanding.

We may not agree to eat together at the end of the day, but at least we can show some respect for each other's table manners, and perhaps even understand that they were not specifically designed to offend us or exclude us. They may do so, of course, just as languages often do. But then, that's what all stories do: they hold some people together and keep others apart.

There's one further step we have to make, whoever and wherever we are. In all our conflicts, we need to find a ceremony that will sanctify the land for everyone who lives on it. I believe that one of the reasons there is so much agitation around environmental issues, especially by young people, is that deep in their hearts they know that pollution is unholy, as well as unhealthy. Part of their outrage has to do with practicalities, of course: clean air and clean water, preserving fish stocks and practising methods of farming that don't poison our food. But part has to do with the sacredness of land and of life.

I keep returning to the experience of aboriginal peoples because it seems to me to provide a lesson for us all. And for all its much-vaunted reputation as an international mediator and peacemaker, it is in this story of natives and newcomers that Canada really has something to offer the world.

Let me set the scene. The body of a dead Indian has been dragged about this continent for centuries, displayed in theatres of desecration that went by the name of Indian removals and native reservations, tribal termination and educational assimilation. All of them produced their own Trail of Tears. All of them destroyed indigenous livelihoods and languages: hundreds of languages—or thousands, depending how you count—have disappeared over the past five hundred years, and at least fifty more are on the brink of extinction right now. All of them involved exercises in cultural genocide premised on that unresolved issue of aboriginal humanity, on a cluster of conflicts over language and livelihood, and on a single metaphor about land, in which a fiction—a story—was created to credit the fact of ownership. We call it "title." It recalls, in a grim way, the sixteenth-century argument about slavery and personhood between Sepulveda and Las Casas. If we have this title, we believe the land—the property—is ours, and that we can do with it what we want.

Remember Ras Kumi saying there are people who think the world is round, and people who think the world is flat, and that they are the same people. In the same way, there is *another* title, one that contradicts this idea of exclusive ownership. We need to find a way of believing them both, just as we believe in both a sun that rises and a sun that remains right where it is.

Actually, we already do, so what I am suggesting should come easily. The other title is sometimes called "underlying" title. We don't think about it from day to day, just as we don't think about the round earth, until we are reminded about our responsibility to the land and to its creator or until the government decides to put a road across our front lawn or build a dam and flood the valley we live in. Then we are made rudely aware of the fact that our title is not quite as true as we thought it was. It is underwritten by a title vested in the nation—for example, the republic (in the United States) or the monarchy (in Canada). It is a legal fiction, of course; but it shapes the facts of life and of the land.

Why should underlying title be vested in the storyline of the settler society? Well, it's our story, is the obvious answer. And we have become so used to telling it that we believe it. But we have forgotten how arbitrary it is; meaningless, we might even say, echoing McLuhan's line about how we build meaning out of meaninglessness. We need to recover a sense of this. We need to reclaim the unbelievability of our belief, and the contradiction between reality and the imagination that lies at its heart. The word "under-lying" itself should help.

The native Americans who live among us and were here before us don't believe our story. But they believe another, which is just as unbelievable, a story of underlying aboriginal title. Actually, they believe several, for the aboriginal stories of underlying title are creation stories which vary from tribe to tribe; or they are covenants comparable to those that bind "chosen people" like Afrikaaners or Israelis or Ulster Scots to their land. Put differently, underlying aboriginal title is Turtle title or Raven title or Coyote title or maybe Mediik title, rather than Crown title. I'm not being facetious here. Underlying title, whatever adjective we apply to it, is a trick, a way of understanding something beyond everyday understanding; but it's a trick the way the theories of science are, or the law, which routinely establish fictions as facts. So why not an aboriginal "trick"? Why not change underlying title back to aboriginal title?

Changing any story about underlying title has powerful implications, of course. It is what the United States did at the time of the Revolution, replacing Crown title with the title of the republic. So this would be revolutionary, grumble some people nervously. Perhaps it would, in the revolutionary way that gave rise to the American republic in the first place. But if you think that particular revolution is over, maybe it would be revolutionary the way the 1994 election of the African National Congress in South Africa was revolutionary. Not such a bad thing. Others complain that it would be a return to the past. Let's get serious. The past is where we live with the settlers' story anyway.

For despite appearances, it is not the conflict between the two sets of stories that is the problem. The problem is our forgetting the contradiction between fact and fiction, the true and the not true, upon which *any* story—including *our* story—depends for its power; and our ignoring the credit upon which any currency—like the currency of ownership, or of government—ultimately depends. Changing to underlying aboriginal title would remind both sides of this. One of the reasons land claims have been so unsuccessful, I believe, is that they don't get at the nature of belief and of credit. *Tulku* and *tjakurrpa* do. So does telling a story in Gitksan. Those of us who speak English (or French, or any other language) understand precisely because we cannot understand.

Some folks will say that taking such a radical step would undo everything that decent people, settler people, have worked for through their own troubled times. But that's nonsense; not the decency or the hard work, but the idea that changing underlying title would undo the good things that have been done. In one sense, it wouldn't change anything at all. People didn't start falling off the earth when everyone agreed that it was really round. Changing to underlying aboriginal title wouldn't mean that an Indian chief could come and sit on my doorstep or walk into my house, any more than the Queen or the president could right now. If they tried, I'd have the courts and Parliament or Congress on my side in an instant, just as I would if the state or its representatives tried to interfere with any of my other rights. There would still be the possibility of expropriation, of course, but that would follow the same procedures, and meet with the same resistance, as at present. Nothing would change if underlying title were aboriginal title. It would be a fiction. The facts of life would remain the same.

And yet of course they would not remain the same, because this new title would constitute a new story and a new society. Our understanding of the land would change. Our understanding of aboriginal peoples would change. Our understanding of ourselves would change. Our sense of the origin and purpose of our nations would change. And underlying title would finally provide a constitutional ceremony of belief in the humanity of aboriginal peoples in the Americas. It would finish the job Las Casas began, which is where we began in Chapter 1.

To grumble about the practicalities of changing to underlying aboriginal title is beside the point. The lawyers would work it out, as they work out many other personifications and paradoxes that characterize our social and economic and political lives. And the descendants of the aboriginal inhabitants of the Americas, the native American peoples, would do what their ancestors have done for millennia: work out new ways of living together with strange people who have strange habits and speak strange languages. There are all sorts of models in settler societies too, from medieval to modern Europe, of how such a change might be achieved, and how contingent sovereignties could be articulated in law and reconciled with existing national constitutions.

If we tell this new story of underlying aboriginal title often enough, we'll get used to it, just as we get used to nursery rhymes and national anthems. At the same time we'll be surprised each time we tell it. It will not be exactly true, any more than our current story is. It will still be a metaphor, a hinge, a trick. But we will say about it the same thing we say about something that happens in a story that could never have happened: "Now it has." And telling this new story in the Americas, where the conflicts have not yet erupted into whole-scale violence (though there have been countless local clashes), would give an example to other communities—in the Middle East, in South Asia, in parts of Africa and in most of Europe—where conflicts over land mask deeper misunderstandings over stories such as this.

There is a song by Bob Marley called "Duppy Conqueror," which begins, "Yes, me friend, me friend, him set me free again." It is about breaking free from the power of a duppy, a ghost or spirit of the dead whose burial rites have been incomplete. The spirit wanders homeless, ready to be captured by others with evil on their minds. Instead of being an ancestral protector, the duppy becomes an evil presence, performing the will of the obeah-men who, in the rhetoric of Marley's song, are the politicians and judges representing the corrupt society of contemporary Babylon. Though the image is located in Jamaican language and beliefs, it conveys a universal warning about the price we all pay, one way or another, for failing to come to terms with our ghosts.

We can all be duppy conquerors and be released from the dread I felt watching the ayatollah or the grief that Martha Demientieff told about before the river released her. We can set the stage for addressing not only the holocaust of slavery and the horror of continuing racism, but also provide that "audience of gods" which Don McKay talked about, laying to rest the atrocity represented by the indigenous dead, those who to this day are forbidden to return to dust, but are scribbled in it. And we can move beyond the archetypal antagonism between the barbaric and the civilized that sustains so many

conflicts around the world. We can replace the theatre of desecration with the theatre of a decent burial.

Until we have done so, the barbarians will continue to be in
charge. And make no mistake: Them is Us. All of us. The barbarians are at the gates, we say. But we forget that they are on
both sides of it. We can call the gate by other names—the
border, the crossroads—but whatever we call it, it is where we
meet. When I went to the Middle East some years ago, I carried
two passports, because the Arabs and the Israelis did not want to
admit that there was only one of me. It worked. I remember
thinking that there is probably two of everyone. We are all, in
some sense, Them and Us. People who think the world is round,
and people who think the world is flat. Same people.

We need to take a cue from mathematics and the sciences
and develop a greater comfort level with contradiction as a way
of life, and a way beyond our most debilitating conflicts. For
while deciding whether Achilles catches the tortoise or whether
we can square the circle may not seem to generate much controversy, it had people at loggerheads for over two thousand
years. And its resolution transformed all of our lives in ways
we hardly realize. And what about that line between the human
and the non-human, or the natural and the unnatural—the line
that troubles us in questions about abortion and euthanasia and
genetic modification—which we are still trying to negotiate?
Suddenly the question "If this is your land, where are your stories?" seems a little simpler.

Which brings us to the grandfather and godmother of
them all, the conflict between creation stories, or between the
so-called "realistic" discoveries of the sciences and "imaginative" inventions of religion and the arts. I hope by now we are
ready to reverse these categories; or at least to acknowledge
the arbitrariness of each. Deliberately or not, such comple-
mentary sets of stories always develop in ways that ensure
their contradiction. *That* is their hold on us.

In the Introduction I spoke of the connection between wonder and wondering, and of how, if we separate them, we can end up with the kind of amazement that is satisfied with the first explanation, or the kind of curiosity that is incapable of genuine surprise. I must admit to some despair at the extent to which we have institutionalized this separation in our schools and colleges and universities. I teach at a university, and I'm constantly asked one question by family and friends, tax collectors and taxi drivers. What do I actually *do* there? To which I have a simple answer: I tell stories. That's what we all do there, in ceremonies of belief and disbelief, of wonder and surprise. We tell stories about evolution or the decline and fall of the Roman Empire; we imagine the drama of a Big Bang or a Great War; we sing songs about justice and freedom or chaos and order. And we make up new stories and songs. We call the old ones teaching, and the new ones research. But whatever we call them, we are in an ancient tradition of elders, experts, eccentrics and enthusiasts, telling tales and singing songs.

I would add one other thing. Many of us, working as scholars and scientists, interrupt our stories so that they don't incarcerate us. Call it what you will—the deconstruction of our narratives or the untelling of our tales or the standing apart from the fray—it helps us maintain our sense of what we are doing and why; of the difference between the yard and the tower, and their ultimate indistinguishability; and of the need to acknowledge both the arbitrariness of all categories and their naturalness. "Give me a place to stand . . . and I will move the world," Archimedes is said to have boasted. We don't want to do that; but we do want to understand—or overstand—the world. The words "school" and "scholarship" come from the Greek word *schole*, which means "leisure." We want to look at the world with the leisure that liberates the mind when it is released from the obligation merely to do things, or to believe things. We want to bring disbelief to bear on our beliefs, so that we recognize their interdependence.

And yet leisure like this conjures up those old questions: "It's all very well for folks to sing songs and tell stories and talk all through the night about whatever comes into their minds and call that work, but it sounds more like play. What about the *real* work of the world? Who's going to do that?"

A fair question; though standing apart, like good scholarship, gives us the ability to decide the meaning and value of that work without losing our foothold in this world. Again, the sciences may help here. Think of a honeycomb. From one perspective, it displays such exquisitely crafted design and economy of construction that we are inclined to see it as an illustration of the bee's extraordinary workmanship. But there is another way of looking at this, in which the bee simply works with material in which an intrinsic economy insists upon itself for reasons that have to do with the mathematics and physics of cell structures and polygon forms rather than the invention of bees.

The philosopher Herbert Simon takes this another step, describing an ant working its way along a beach. The surface is uneven, and the ingenuity of the ant in navigating across it is wonderful to behold. Except that the wonder, Simon suggests, might be in the beach rather than the ant. Looked at this way, it is the beach that is complex; the ant is just an ant, barely sophisticated enough to use the beach to find its way. In each case, it is the wonder itself that is important.

Any story that purports to provide an explanation of phenomena hovers between imaginative agency and the nature of reality. The Biblical story of creation has both a teleology (God's purpose, the product of divine "force") and a mechanism (six days of creation, Adam and Eve, a sequence of events). So do all the creation stories I know of. In a similar way, the various stories of the flood, including Mediik's and Noah's, are both illustrations of a greater purpose and precipitated by specific processes, or causes and effects. Asking whether the purposes and processes that we perceive in such stories are *really* there is like asking whether the Greeks believed in their myths. Yes and no. We need to keep this contradiction alive when we think of other people's stories as well as our own, and be careful not to discredit either the yes *or* the no.

There's a final story I want to tell from Gitksan territory. It confuses perspectives without jeopardizing their independence; it confounds those who would make tidy choices; and it is one more answer to the question "If this is your land, where are your stories?" The whole community had gathered to discuss the future of local fishing, important for both its cultural and commercial value. There were both natives and newcomers there, but they shared a sense of ceremony: the ceremony of fishing, a livelihood both ancient and modern; and the ceremony of witnessing to its importance.

One member of the group went to the microphone and in deeply moving language sang a praise song to the early-morning pleasures of fishing in the Kispiox, the river running through the ancient homeland of the Gitksan where Mediik had brought down the mountain. He described the first light coming as a quiet surprise over the mountains and down through the trees that sheltered the waters of the river; the mist hovering over the deep tranquility of its upstream eddies and the pools below the rapids; the sure and purposeful flow of the river as it went on its way to the ocean hundreds of miles away. He told how the salmon who had come home to the valley again this year rose up from their resting places to take the finely crafted flies and to offer themselves to those who were there in a good way, by which he meant those who came humbly, with skills it takes a lifetime to learn properly and an openness to the spirits of the place and the wonder of that unpredictable moment when the connection is made. He talked about how the line between the sacred and the profane is, as the Creek poet Joy Harjo once said, as thin as fishing line.

Another man then came up to speak. He too began his story in the early morning, but his eyes were on the surface, dead calm as the light broke from the edges of the horizon and spread along the nearer shore. Hardly a breath out there, and only a couple of creases where the lines touched. A few ripples, in a peacefulness that was part of the creator's plan. Then a few dimples on the surface . . . one here, one there, another one way off to the side. Then smooth as silk again . . . but before long some more snicks, like small flies bouncing off glass. And they really *were* flies, and the fish came up for them, just breaking the top of the water, which by now rippled like galvanized roofing. Soon the whole surface of the sea was alive, the water teeming and the lines tightening as the purse seiner hauled in its bounty just offshore where the salmon ranged in another season. Another kind of gift, the salmon of the open sea surrendering to the people as they had for thousands of years.

It was a strange confusion of stories. The first was told by a newcomer to the region, a latter-day cowboy and sports fisherman who loved following the frontier and fly fishing but who was doing what the Gitksan had done since time immemorial, using different methods but the same sense of ceremony; while the other, wearing the working slickers of a commercial fisherman, was the brother of Neil Sterritt, the Gitksan leader who played such an important role in matching the story of Mediik the grizzly with the geologist's core sample. Neil told me that his brother's eloquence, telling of the life that brought him a living in settler society, was something he had never heard before—or never listened to.

There may have been spirits of place that each didn't know about; but both the cowboy and the Indian came together in their deep respect for the land, and for a language of praise and thanksgiving. They spoke to persuade others that in order to protect the land, and the livelihoods and leisure that depend upon it, they had to find a language that would catch the element of strangeness, of surprise, of sorrow and sudden joy at its centre. They spoke to save the land from being divided up into sheep units and polluted by unfriendly spirits. They left disagreeing about almost everything else, including whose land they were protecting. But they were one in wonder, and like the Gitksan elder and the government foresters, they came to an agreement on how to protect some things of meaning and value in their lives.

During the Middle Ages, institutions of higher learning divided knowledge not into the sciences and the arts, nor into the useful and the useless, but into house law (the Latin word was *economia*) and star law (*astronomia*). The first was concerned with the things of the earth and their particular orderings, the second with the sun and the moon and the stars and the design and purpose of the universe. And for each they composed stories and songs, which in due course became the great books and the great truths of that culture. They understood that these stories and songs had power—the power of the imagination—both to protect them from reality and to bring them closer to it. They knew that stories and songs were both a walk in the storm and a shelter from it.

By confusing the categories of reality and the imagination, and the finite and the infinite, these medieval scholars, singers and storytellers confounded those who thought that it was necessary to choose between them. As we have seen over and over again in this book, it is not.

That is why ceremonies are so important. They draw our attention to the difference between the natural and the human, the barbaric and the civilized, the secular and the sacred, and then they show us how to ignore it. They give us a way of saying "I believe" when we are not sure; of getting consolation when our hearts are broken; of watching spring come in when we know that it will never again come for us; of understanding every word when the words do not make sense. They take place in moments of grace, but these moments are always precarious and often downright dangerous. They build up and break down our sense of who we are and where we belong. And they keep us in a state of wonder. The common ground I have talked about is neither a spot of land nor a set of stories. It is a state of mind in which we accept that the categories of reality and the imagination are like the categories of Them and Us.

Riddles and charms bring words and the world together and test one against the other to see which gives way. That is what we are constantly doing with both land and with stories. That is what the question that forms the title of this book does. In a riddle, it is language that gives, while the world stays just as it is—with cherries that have stones and cherry blossoms that do not. In a charm, it is the world that changes—if only for that moment when we sing our national anthem or recite our creed or repeat our creation story. Riddles highlight the categories of language and life; charms collapse them. Neither does away with them.

This book has a modest ambition: to give the reader a sense of how important it is to come together in a new understanding of the power and the paradox of stories. If we can do this, I believe we will be able to understand how the contradictions that are part of the art of storytelling are also part of the nature of our lives and our conflicts over land, and how the way in which we divide up the world into Them and Us is inseparable from the way we understand stories themselves. Dividing the world up into Them and Us is inevitable. But choosing between is like choosing between reality and the imagination, or between being marooned on an island and drowning in the sea. Deadly, and ultimately a delusion.

This is where ceremonies of belief come into the picture. They are always caught up in contradiction. Like calculus, they finesse the question of whether Achilles will ever catch the tortoise by saying, "Now he does." They take us to a place where things happen that don't. They give us the confidence to reject the choice between words and the world. And they put us on common ground.

Like home, it is at the centre of contradiction. It is a place where what we have in common is neither true nor untrue, a place where we come together in agreement not about what to believe but about what it is to believe. It is the ground shared by Them and Us, and it is the answer to the question "If this is your land, where are your stories?" On common ground.

INTRODUCTION

The title story was told to me by Peter Usher, though I have heard it since in many different forms and languages around the world.

I use a wide range of words to refer to the aboriginal peoples of the world, reflecting different times and places and practices. Some of them, like the names of individuals and communities in their indigenous languages, are currently correct (though the spellings are inevitably imprecise); some terms, like "Inuit" and "Eskimo," or "aboriginals" and "Indians," are correct in some countries but not in others; and some, like "natives" and "Bushmen," are less correct these days. I use them all on occasion. I apologize if I offend anyone by doing so; but I hope the stories make amends.

CHAPTER ONE

Marshall McLuhan made his remark in *The Gutenberg Galaxy* (1962). The account of Bushmen yodelling is from an essay by Deirdre Hansen in *Miscast: Negotiating the Presence of the Bushmen*, edited by Pippa Skotnes (1996); one settler reported that the sounds "resembled nothing so much as a herd of year-ling calves just turned out of the cowshed."

The details of the Delgamuukw case are available in a book of excerpts, cartoons and commentary from the trial compiled by Don Monet and Skanu'u (Ardythe Wilson), *Colonialism on Trial: Indigenous Land Rights and the Gitksan and Wet'suwet'en Sovereignty Case* (1992), and in the Supreme Court judgment of December 11, 1997. There is a fine essay by Leslie Pinder, "The Carriers of No" (1991); and a study of the trial by Dara Culhane, *The Pleasure of the Crown* (1998).

The most complete discussion of the debate between Las Casas and Sepulveda is by Lewis Hanke in *Aristotle and the American Indians* (1959) and *All Mankind Is One* (1974), though it is mentioned in most of the histories of early settlement and has been given new life by Sylvia Wynter in two essays titled "New Seville" and "The Conversion Experience of Bartolomé de Las Casas," which appeared in *Jamaica Journal* in 1984.

Charlie Tjungurrayi's greeting was recounted in an essay by Neil Murray, "Home/Away" (*Sydney Bulletin Literary Supplement* [November, 1983]).

Wordsworth's view of language is outlined in the third of his *Essays upon Epitaphs* (1810); Coleridge's in *Biographia Literaria* (1817); and Benjamin Lee Whorf's theory of linguistic relativity is described in a collection of his essays, *Language, Thought and Reality,* edited by John Carroll (1964).

The identification of Indian languages as barbaric is a set piece of the Americas, and was a fundamental premise of Indian schools; getting children away from their families was the logical first step. My discussion of the conventional wisdom about oral and written traditions is taken from Walter Ong's regrettably influential *Orality and Literacy* (1982); a more balanced view than Ong's can be found in David R. Olson's *The World on Paper* (1994).

The late chief Jacob Thomas told me his story about reciting the Great Law of the Haudenosaunee in translation.

Matthew Arnold's *Culture and Anarchy* (1869) began as a lecture that he delivered as Professor of Poetry at Oxford in 1867, called "Culture and Its Enemies."

CHAPTER TWO

The description of the Montana constitution is from Daniel Kemmis's *Community and the Politics of Place* (1990). Crowfoot is quoted in Hugh Dempsey's *Crowfoot: Chief of the Blackfeet* (1972).

George Grey's account is from his *Journals of Two Expeditions of Discovery* (1841), quoted in Henry Reynolds, *The Other Side of the Frontier: Aboriginal Resistance to the European Invasion of Australia* (1982); and "There goes the neighbourhood" is from a cartoon I saw in Australia in the mid-1980s . . . but I suspect indigenous people have been saying that for centuries.

Sitting Bull's speech is recorded in *Great Documents in American Indian History*, edited by Wayne Moquin and Charles Van Doren (1973).

I first came across the Majorcan storytellers in "Linguistics and Poetics" (1958), an essay by Roman Jakobsen. The definition of infinity is both old and new: I heard it from my mother; and Eli Maor attributes it to an unidentified schoolboy in *To Infinity and Beyond: A Cultural History of the Infinite* (1991), a book from which I have learned much.

Some of the details in my account of cowboy life, including the quotation from the fence-cutting Alberta cowboy, are from Richard Slatta's splendid *Cowboys of the Americas* (1990); and while cowboy humour is legendary, there are some good examples collected by Stan Hoig in *Humor of the American Cowboy* (1958). Theodore Roosevelt made his comment in his first annual message in 1901; the Meriam Report was titled

The Problem of Indian Administration (1928); and Reeseman Fryer's description of the trauma of sheep units is from his unpublished monograph, *Erosion, Poverty and Dependency: Memoir of My Time in Navajo Service, 1933–1942* (1986), kindly made available to me by his daughter, Ann Van Fossen.

CHAPTER THREE

The Cornish proverb is quoted by Tony Harrison in his poem "National Trust" (*The School of Eloquence* [1978]). John Locke's remark is from his *Two Treatises of Civil Government* (1690); it is quoted by Jean-Jacques Rousseau in his "Discourse on the Origin of Inequality," translated by G. D. H. Cole.

George Watts told me later that he was quoting Bill Wilson, another chief from the West Coast; I like to think they were speaking as one.

Coleridge's declaration is from *The Friend* (1809). Hugh Morgan's comments were made in a speech in May 1984; Lang Hancock was quoted in Adam Shoemaker's *Black Words, White Page: Aboriginal Literature, 1929–1988* (1989) from Michael Coyne and Leigh Edwards' *Oz Factor: Who's Doing What in Australia* (1980); and the Minister of Aboriginal Affairs who spoke with corresponding candour about the terrorism of settler society was Clive Holding. Sir William Johnson's letter to the Earl of Shelburne is quoted in the first of three essays by Duncan Campbell Scott in *Canada and Its Provinces,* edited by Adam Shortt and Arthur G. Doughty (1913–14); Andrew Jackson's remarks are in D'Arcy McNickle's *Native American Tribalism* (1973). The quotation by Lewis Cass is from an article he wrote in *North American Review* in 1830, later published as a book titled *Considerations on the Present State of the Indians and Their Removal to the West of the Mississippi,* in which he lamented "that a few naked wandering barbarians should stay the march of cultivation and improvement." Robert J. Merritt's *The Cake Man* was first performed and published in Sydney in 1978.

The text of Woody Guthrie's song, and his description of the places where he sang, is from a script composed of his writings and lyrics, titled *From California to the New York Island* and published by the Guthrie Children's Trust Fund in New York (1960). Gary Holthaus wrote about the natural world and sacred places in 1998 in an unpublished essay.

CHAPTER FOUR

Seamus Heaney's line is from "The Tollund Man" (*Wintering Out* [1972]); Kamau Brathwaite's from "Postlude/Home" (*Rights of Passage* [1967], the first of his trilogy, *The Arrivants* [1973]). The Mexican ballad is mentioned in a commentary on "The Big Rock Candy Mountain" in Alan Lomax's *Folk Songs of North America* (1960). "By the Rivers of Babylon" is Psalm 137. Ernest Renan made his remark in a lecture he gave in 1882, translated by Wanda Romer Taylor as "What Is a Nation?" (1996).

W. E. H. Stanner's description of the homeless is from his monograph *After the Dreaming* (1968), the text of his Australian Broadcasting Corporation Boyer lecture; it was a series that also included Bernard Smith's *The Spectre of Truganini* (1980), from which I have taken my description (in chapter 5) of Truganini's last days.

My characterization of Odysseus is indebted to Bernard Knox's introduction to Robert Fagles' translation of *The Odyssey* (1996), from which I have also drawn all my quotations. The last line of *The Iliad* that I quote in chapter 2 is from S. H. Butcher and Andrew Lang's 1879 prose translation, which was standard fare when I was in school. The Robert Service ballad is titled "The Shooting of Dan McGrew"

(*Songs of a Sourdough* [1907]), though I knew it by heart long before I read it in a book.

The Doukhobor history is from Doukhobor friends, and from George Woodcock and Ivan Avakumovic's *Doukhobors* (1968); the description of psalm singing is from *Songs of the Doukhobor*, edited by Kenneth Peacock (1970).

CHAPTER FIVE

Derek Walcott's cautionary words are from the title poem of *Sea Grapes* (1976) and "The Schooner *Flight*" (*The Star-Apple Kingdom* [1979]); Don McKay's poem is from *Apparatus* (1997); Iain Crichton Smith asks his question, and others too, in "Shall Gaelic Die?" (*Selected Poems* [1985]). The translation from Dante's *Inferno* is by Mark Musa (1971); Hart Crane's lines are from "Dublinesque" (*White Buildings* [1926]); Patrick Lane's poem is "Elephant" (*Poems New and Selected* [1978]); and Tennyson's is "Morte d'Arthur."

The story of aboriginal resettlement has been told by Dick Leichleitner Japanangka and Pam Nathan in *Pmere Arlaltyewele: Settle Down Country* (1983).

I have focused the story of the ≠Khomani on individuals in the community, but a number of outsiders have been involved in negotiating and facilitating their return to the Kalahari, especially Roger Chennells, Nigel Crawhall and Hugh Brody. Brody's *Other Side of Eden: Hunters, Farmers and the Shaping of the World* (2000) comes out of work we did together there, and from his own remarkable travels over the past thirty years. I have learned much from working with him. The transcriptions and translations of N|u that I quote are by Levi Namaseb.

Elsie Vaalbooi died on October 6, 2002. More than five hundred people attended her funeral, including all of the N|u-speaking elders. She had asked to be buried on San land, but after a bitter dispute between families she was buried outside Rietfontein.

CHAPTER SIX

"One Misty, Moisty Morning" is included in Richard Scarry's *Best Mother Goose Ever* (1964). Robert Frost's poem is "Stopping by Woods on a Snowy Evening" (*New Hampshire* [1923]). Mary Warnock's spirited defence of beautiful unordinary language is from her essay "Ancient and Modern" in an issue of *PN Review* titled "Crisis for Cranmer and King James," edited by Michael Schmidt (1979).

Northrop Frye's comment about the mysterious world between is and is not from *The Secular Scripture* (1976); comes his discussion of the ghost in Hamlet and the discovery of zero are from *The Anatomy of Criticism* (1957). Bertrand Russell's remark about mathematicians is quoted in Lucienne Felix, *The Modern Aspect of Mathematics*, translated by Julius H. Hlavaty and Fancille H. Hlavaty (1960), as are Leopold Kronecker's and Charles Hermite's comments about irrational and transcendental numbers. I have greatly benefited from Robert Denham's *Journey Through Genius: The Great Theorems of Mathematics* (1990) in my discussion of imaginary numbers, Georg Cantor's theory of sets, and calculus. My thoughts on tracking were encouraged by Louis Liebenberg's *Art of Tracking: The Origin of Science* (1990).

I first read about "not ants, but ants" in an essay by N. Scott Momaday, who identified the individual only as a friend. Larry Evers said he thought it might be Barre Toelken, who confirmed to me that it was indeed his story.

Ian Tyson's song is titled "The Gift" and can be found on his album *Cowboyography* (1986). The fable of Chuang Chou is from *The Complete Works of Chuang Tzu*, translated by Burton Watson (1968).

CHAPTER SEVEN

Charles Tomlinson's line is from his poem "A Meditation on John Constable" (*Seeing Is Believing* [1960]); Oscar Wilde's from his essay "The Decay of Lying" (1891). Derek Walcott's *Another Life* was published as a book-length poem, and his prose comments are from "The Muse of History," first given as a lecture in 1976. There is a wonderful account of the Chauvet paintings in *Dawn of Art: The Chauvet Cave* by Jean-Marie Chauvet, Eliette Brunel Deschamps and Christian Hillaire (1996). I found the anecdote about Jacobsen in J. B. Leishman and Stephen Spender's introduction to the *Duino Elegies* of Rainer Maria Rilke (1939).

Umberto Eco's sly remark about lying is in his *Theory of Semiotics* (1976); and Dan Yashinsky's about faking it is from an unpublished essay, "Lives of the Storytellers." John Polanyi's testimonial is from his essay "The Magic of Science" (in *The Canadian Federation for the Humanities Bulletin* [1994]).

The story about the Gitksan elder was told to me by Neil Sterritt.

The anecdote from *Marathon Man* is repeated in a number of Olivier biographies. The anniversary saga of Halldór Laxness is from "What Was Before the Saga: A Jubilee Discourse," published in *The American Scandinavian Review* (1974). The gospel passages are from John 5:31 and 8:14. The full title of Wallace Stegner's book is *Wolf Willow: A History, a Story, and a Memory of the Last Plains Frontier* (1962).

CHAPTER EIGHT

Mortimo Planno's remarks are from my conversations with him, and from the text of *The Earth Most Strangest Man* (discussed in chapter 9), which was transcribed from the handwritten original by Lambros Comitas and given back to Ras Kumi in a ceremony at the University of the West Indies in Jamaica in 1997. I published excerpts in an issue of *Index on Censorship* on "Tribes: Battle for Land and Language" that I co-edited in 1996; the full text has circulated in the Rastafarian communities, but not far beyond. The Rastafarian interpretation of the Bible as what Coleridge once called "a science of realities" mirrors the Passover injunction that in each generation Jews *realize* (rather than "merely" imagine) that they themselves came out of Egypt, and enact this in the Seder.

The riddle that rattled Homer provides the epigraph to W. S. Merwin's book of poems *The Lice* (1967); it has been refreshed by Robert Finley in his essay "The Riddle's Charm" (*Dalhousie Review* [Autumn 1997]). The particular poems by Michael Ondaatje and Lorna Goodison that I have in mind are "The Cinnamon Peeler" (*Running in the Family* [1982]) and "Guinea Woman" (*I Am Becoming My Mother* [1986]), though the metaphors appear throughout their work.

For Cantor's own account of his idea, see *Contributions to the Founding of the Theory of Transfinite Numbers*, translated by Philip E. B. Jourdain (1915), and Hans Hahn's lecture "Infinity," delivered under the auspices of the famed Vienna Circle and published in James R. Newman's *World of Mathematics*, vol. 3 (1956). Bertrand Russell's resolution of the paradox of Tristam Shandy is from his essay "Mathematics and the Metaphysicians" (*Mysticism and Logic* [1929]). I found useful discussions of aphorisms in "The Limit of Limits" by Linda Orr (*Symbolism and Modern Literature: Essays in Honour of Wallace Fowlie*, ed. Marcel Teitel [1978]) and Rosalie Colie's *Paradoxica Epidemica: The Renaissance Tradition of Paradox* [1966]). Ernest Newman's remark is from an essay he wrote on Oscar Wilde in 1895. The story about the Dorze is told by Paul Veyne in the preface to *Did the Greeks Believe in Their Myths?* translated by Paula Wissing (1988).

CHAPTER NINE

The BBC documentary was called "Another Country—As a Tale That Is Told." It was produced by Kate McAll, and broadcast on Radio 3 in November 2002. "Do Not Stand at My Grave and Weep" is published in *The Nation's Favourite Poems*, edited by Griff Rhys Jones (1996).

There is a good discussion of Rastafarian language in Velma Pollard's *Dread Talk* (1994); the best account of Rastafarian traditions is Barry Chevannes's *Rastafari: Roots and Ideology* (1995). I am indebted for some thoughts on Rastafari and metaphor to Hugh Hodges.

Wordsworth's up-to-date polemic on popular culture is from his preface to the *Lyrical Ballads* (1800); Derek Walcott's lines are from his poem "Forests of Europe," dedicated to Joseph Brodsky (*The Star-Apple Kingdom*). Plutarch's quotation is from John Lubbock's *Pleasures of Life* (1887), in which Lubbock first set out the list that became the foundation for the Great Books programs of the twentieth century that I mentioned in chapter 2. Lubbock proposed and (with George Routledge) published these books in sturdy inexpensive volumes for the Workers and Mechanics Institute.

CHAPTER TEN

Gary Holthaus describes his grandfather's milking stool in an unpublished essay "The Nature Conservancy: Habitat for a Sustainable Life" (1998). Edgar Allan Poe's cheerful reflections on human psychology are from his "Philosophy of Composition" (1848).

Martha Demientieff told me her story in Seattle, where we were at a meeting together. She was homesick, down south; but one morning she came in for breakfast all smiles. She had seen a raven, who had told her that everything was all right, and that he had come to keep her company. "Make prayers to the raven," she said, bringing us together in belief—for that was the title of the anthropologist Richard Nelson's then recently published book on the Koyukon people of Alaska, which she and I both admired.

Galileo and Poincaré are quoted in Morris Kline, *Mathematics in Western Culture* (1953); Gauss in Robert Denham; and Einstein in Eli Maor. My discussion of Cusanus was helped by Peter Salm's *Pinpoint of Eternity: European Literature in Search of the All-Encompassing Moment* (1986).

Edward Baugh's poem is from *A Tale from the Rainforest* (1988); and Galeano's essay is translated by Mariana Valverde in *The Writer and Human Rights* (1983). There is a good description of the legacy of Boethius in Jerry Martin's "Universals and Particulars: A Tale of Two Places" (*Humanities in the South* [1991]). Jonathan Swift's acid remark is the first of his "Thoughts on Various Subjects," a collection of aphorisms published in *Miscellanies* (1711).

Charles Darwin's complaint was added to his third edition of *On the Origin of Species* (1861); D'Arcy Thompson's book was edited in an abridged form by John Tylor Bonner in 1966, from which Kepler's quotation is taken. There is an elegant discussion of time in Stephen Jay Gould's *Time's Arrow/Time's Cycle: Myth and Metaphor in the Discovery of Geological Time* (1987); and Vine Deloria Jr. described the buffalo hunt in an essay "Ethnoscience and Indian Realities" (*Winds of Change* [1992]). J. B. S. Haldane's distinction between science and religion is from "Science and Reality as Art Forms" (*The New Criticism*, ed. Edwin B. Burgum [1930]).

CHAPTER ELEVEN

The story of Mediik was told in the Delgamuukw case.

The phrase "seeing with an innocent eye" is adapted from John Ruskin's discussion of the "innocence of the eye" in *The Elements of Drawing* (1856), elaborated by E. H. Gombrich in *Art and Illusion* (1962). The translation of Confucius's analect 13:3 is by Roger T. Ames and Henry Rosemont, Jr. in *The Analects of Confucius: A Philosophical Translation* (1999).

The most serious engagement with the issue of underlying title has been by Michael Asch and Norman Zlotkin in their essay "Affirming Aboriginal Title: A New Basis for Comprehensive Claims Negotiations" (*Aboriginal and Treaty Rights in Canada*, ed. Michael Asch [1997]), though Asch has been mapping the territory for a long time as an anthropologist in the north of Canada, and in the worldwide geography of songs and stories fostered by his father, Moses Asch, the founder of Folkways Records. The Smithsonian Folkways Archive has now taken on the role of house-worrier of this heritage, with Michael Asch very much involved.

The honeycomb is from D'Arcy Thompson. Herbert Simon's anecdote is from *The Sciences of the Artificial* (1969); I first came across it in an essay by Brian Langille and Arthur Ripstein, "Strictly Speaking, It Went Without Saying" (*Legal Theory* [1996]). Joy Harjo's line is from "Fishing" (*The Woman Who Fell from the Sky* [1994]).

The story of the two fishermen in Gitksan territory was told to me by Neil Sterritt.

ACKNOWLEDGMENTS

My greatest debts are to my children, Sarah, Geoff and Meg; and to my wife, Lorna Goodison.

I would also like to give thanks, too little and sadly too late, to Edith Cowdry Chamberlin (1899–1986), Edward Eugene Chamberlin (1903–1996) and Jane Clement Chamberlin (1945–1998).

And then the doors open onto a wide crowd of friends and fellow travellers, most of whom I must thank in one sweeping gesture. I do want to mention a few special mentors and minders: Margaret Williams, Tony Parker-Jervis, Jack Cowdry, Ted Zinkan, Bettie Vayda, John Hulcoop, Felp Priestley, Northrop Frye, Kathleen Coburn, Philip Sherlock, Fred Morgan, Tom Berger, and closest of all, my sister Liz and Bob Food, who first brought me to Africa nearly forty years ago. The Connaught Fund of the University of Toronto supported me very generously over several years. And there are friends who helped me in particular ways while I was writing this book. Some are acknowledged in the Notes; others include Michael Asch, Eddie Baugh, Avie Bennett, Barry Chevannes, Brian Corman, Britt Ellis, Lowell Fiet, Len Findlay, Bryan and Carol Finlay, Kim Gertler, Sander Gilman, Miles Goodison and the Goodison clan, Gary Holthaus, Mike Ingram, Richard Landon, Mark McLean, Dorik Mechau, Jean Morriset, Heather Munroe-Blum, John and Barb Murray, Tak Nakajima, Levi Namaseb, Rex Nettleford, Rob Prichard, John Robinson, Richard Sanger, Carolyn Servid, Edgard Sienaert, Jean Smith,

Tim and Nalini Stewart, John Straley and John Stubbs, Barry Watson and Dian Watson. And finally, my thanks to those who put me up—and sometimes held me up—when I went walkabout: John Burns, Paddy Stewart, Adam Shoemaker, Hugh Brody, Stephen Regan, Patrick Saul and Elaine Melbourne.

Jennifer Glossop was an enormous help during a difficult period of rewriting; Jane McWhinney, Noelle Zitzer and Angelika Glover listened closely and edited carefully; Barney Gilmore prepared the index with encouraging enthusiasm; and Deirdre Molina kept us on schedule. Scott Richardson brought his generous and judicious imagination to bear on the design, especially the cover. My thanks to them, and to their genial colleagues at Knopf Canada who brought the book to life.

Ramsay Derry got me going, as he has so often; Janet Irving kept me going, as she has so often; Kate McAll encouraged me to speak out; and Louise Dennys believed me when I did. I owe her this book, and them all my deepest gratitude.

J. EDWARD CHAMBERLIN is Professor of English and Comparative Literature at the University of Toronto. Previously Poetry Editor of *Saturday Night* magazine and senior advisor to the Mackenzie Valley Pipeline Inquiry and the Royal Commission on Aboriginal Peoples, he has worked extensively on native land claims in Canada, the United States, Africa and Australia. His books include *The Harrowing of Eden: White Attitudes Towards Native Americans* (1975), *Ripe was the Drowsy Hour: The Age of Oscar Wilde* (1977) and *Come Back to Me My Language: Poetry and the West Indies* (1993).

Pierre Simon Fournier le jeune, who designed the type used in this book, was both an originator and a collector of types. His services to the art of print communication were his design of letters, his creation of ornaments and initials, and his standardization of type sizes. His types are old style in character and sharply cut. In 1764 and 1766 he published his *Manuel typographique*, a treatise on the history of French types and printing, on typefounding in all its details, and on what many consider his most important contribution to the printed word—the measurement of type by the point system.